UNIVERSAL

Praise for

It was only a matter of time before a clever publisher realized that there is an audience for whom Exile on Main Street or Electric Ladyland are as significant and worthy of study as The Catcher in the Rye or Middlemarch ... The series ... is freewheeling and eclectic, ranging from minute rock-geek analysis to idiosyncratic personal celebration—*The New York Times Book Review*

Ideal for the rock geek who thinks liner notes just aren't enough—*Rolling Stone*

One of the coolest publishing imprints on the planet—*Bookslut*

These are for the insane collectors out there who appreciate fantastic design, well-executed thinking, and things that make your house look cool. Each volume in this series takes a seminal album and breaks it down in startling minutiae. We love these. We are huge nerds—*Vice*

A brilliant series ... each one a work of real love—*NME* (UK) Passionate, obsessive, and smart—*Nylon*

Religious tracts for the rock 'n' roll faithful—*Boldtype*

[A] consistently excellent series—*Uncut* (UK)

We ... aren't naive enough to think that we're your only source for reading about music (but if we had our way ... watch out). For those of you who really like to know everything there is to know about an album, you'd do well to check out Bloomsbury's "33 1/3" series of books—*Pitchfork*

For almost 20 years, the 33-and-a-Third series of music books has focused on individual albums by acts well known (Bob Dylan, Nirvana, Abba, Radiohead), cultish (Neutral Milk Hotel, Throbbing Gristle, Wire) and many levels in-between. The range of music and their creators defines "eclectic", while the writing veers from freewheeling to acutely insightful. In essence, the books are for the music fan who (as Rolling Stone noted) "thinks liner notes just aren't enough."—*The Irish Times*

For reviews of individual titles in the series, please visit our blog at 333sound.com and our website at http://www.bloomsbury.com/musicandsoundstudies

Follow us on Twitter: @333books

Like us on Facebook: https://www.facebook.com/33.3books

For a complete list of books in this series, see the back of this book.

Forthcoming in the series:

Universal Mother

Adele Bertei

BLOOMSBURY ACADEMIC
NEW YORK • LONDON • OXFORD • NEW DELHI • SYDNEY

BLOOMSBURY ACADEMIC
Bloomsbury Publishing Inc
1385 Broadway, New York, NY 10018, USA
50 Bedford Square, London, WC1B 3DP, UK
29 Earlsfort Terrace, Dublin 2, Ireland

BLOOMSBURY, BLOOMSBURY ACADEMIC and the Diana logo are trademarks
of Bloomsbury Publishing Plc

First published in the United States of America 2025

Library of Congress Cataloging-in-Publication Data
Names: Bertei, Adele, author.
Title: Universal mother / Adele Bertei.
Other titles: Sinead O'Connor's Universal mother
Description: [1.] | New York: Bloomsbury Academic, 2025. |
Series: 33 1/3 | Includes bibliographical references.
Identifiers: LCCN 2024026834 (print) | LCCN 2024026835 (ebook) |
ISBN 9798765106914 (paperback) | ISBN 9798765106921 (ebook) |
ISBN 9798765106938 (pdf)
Subjects: LCSH: O'Connor, Sinéad. Universal mother. |
O'Connor, Sinéad–Political activity. | Popular music–1991-2000–History and
criticism. | Adult child sexual abuse victims.
Classification: LCC ML420.O297 B47 2025 (print) | LCC ML420.O297 (ebook) |
DDC 782.42164092–dc23/eng/20240703
LC record available at https://lccn.loc.gov/2024026834
LC ebook record available at https://lccn.loc.gov/2024026835

ISBN: PB: 979-8-7651-0691-4
ePDF: 979-8-7651-0693-8
eBook: 979-8-7651-0692-1

Series: 33 1/3

Typeset by Deanta Global Publishing Services, Chennai, India
Printed and bound in Great Britain

To find out more about our authors and books visit www.bloomsbury.com and
sign up for our newsletters.

for dama
and Maya
and for John.

thank you for listening
and for loving
her

Contents

I'm the voice of dead people.

I'm the interpreter of lost songs.

—Meryl Streep,

speaking about Bertolt Brecht and
Margarete Steffin's Mother Courage[1]

Preface and Disclaimer

High-voltage tip-off for my dear muso brothers who prefer to sink their teeth into the man-mayo of the usual rock criticism; this book is *Ganza*.[1] It's a book misogynists may write off as feminist doggerel. Sinéad O'Connor's lyrics were sometimes described so. Like her, I will say things people think yet are petrified of voicing out loud for fear of persecution in a censorial moment that feels too much like the American Inquisition. I'm writing in Sinéad's honor and in honor of the women without voices, those gone and remaining, and I will happily disgrace myself by speaking of the subconscious and of spiritualism. This fire-breathing dragon who loved us with a warrior's passion lived a public feminism germane to *Universal Mother*, a feminism especially relevant to the sorry

---

[1] Ganza is a neologism for a feminized "gonzo" style of journalism, gonzo first attributed to Hunter S. Thompson and taken up by Lester Bangs, Terry Southern, and other male writers. A first-person participatory style, it uses social critique, political satire, sarcasm, and exaggeration. Women's journalism can also be prankish and belligerent, hence *Ganza*. Ganzá is also a Brazilian rattle, a percussion instrument made of a canister filled with metal balls, beads, and pebbles, this latter description being closer akin to an unrestrained female tongue.

state of our present world. That is, even though I will try my very best to go lightly, this book is feminist as fuck.

You are holding a book of feeling. I *feel* Sinéad and this LP deeply. I feel her and the songs in the genes I have inherited from my Irish mother's side, the generational trauma of Irish women and of that emerald island through the ages. My own trauma seeds the pages as well; with my mother, with abuse, and with the Babylonian music business. Academia will never do her justice, with its tensions toward disregarding empirical wisdom, ignoring the working class unless analyzing it to death (for whom does that serve?), and its scoffing at spirit. O'Connor was an otherworldly gemstone. Her music is humid with anima, not a great match for intellectual settings where an elitist lexicon masks the ache of the womb-heart. Sinéad was self-taught, extremely intelligent, funny as hell and had the mouth of a sailor. She didn't give two fucks. She dedicated *Universal Mother* as a prayer from Ireland, with love and gratitude to her sister Eimear and her son Jake. It is her prayer and her contrition toward healing. Yet within her vulnerable heart were cracks she'd never mend on the search for God's mercy.

The above nattering about academia is hardly meant as a dismissal of the intellect, but instead, is an ask for a consideration that there might be a more imaginative, more generous form of intellect that requires a closer relationship with feeling and spirit as opposed to an MFA-fueled one-upmanship that buries humans in lifelong debt and is boundaried. Elitist. And yet, I want to describe Sinéad's musical language as a "hermeneutic" of loving resistance, because I love the word. It sounds mystical. And Sinéad's was a mystical battle cry against oppression in its many guises.

Women of O'Connor's generation, of our mother's and grandmother's and backwards, were trapped inside the barbed wire-topped walls of the father language and its erasure of women's spirit and power. You had to engage in some mighty magical thinking to traverse those walls and justify your womanly existence as a sovereign being on this planet. As of this writing, the entrapment continues, overt and insidious, painting women as subordinate, our bodies controlled by men who make laws and the women supporting their own subjugation.

While commencing the writing of this book in the summer of 2023, the news arrived that Sinéad O'Connor had died. The irony of the LP title she was working on before she passed, *No Veteran Dies Alone*, constricts the heart.

Someone called the police at 11:18 p.m. on Wednesday, July 26 reporting an unresponsive woman in the SE24 area of London. The Gardai (police) immediately ruled out foul play, and the coroner's report (released five months later in January 2024, allegedly due to a backlog of deaths during COVID) said that she died of natural causes. In July 2024, the *Irish Independent* reported she had died from COPD and asthma. She was a fifty-six-year-old chain-smoker. That Sinéad died of a broken heart is just as probable as suicide would have been for her, or the many other ways she may have ended her journey of "sailing on this terrible ocean."[2] My schizophrenic mother

---

[2] Sinéad O'Connor, "A Perfect Indian," *Universal Mother*.

smoked three packs a day and died of a heart attack cause by a blood clot due to COPD. My maternal Irish grandmother, a smoker, died after suffering a series of heart attacks. And what is a heart attack, if not *a terrible broken heart*?[3]

She did not commit suicide, although she often spoke of it. Not as often as she spoke of her children being more important than anything else in her life. More important than her music. Sinéad's four children were the vertical posts in the guardrail preventing her leap over the parapet, which she claims to have attempted eight times or more. Was the son who cut his own life short, Shane Lunny, the child who needed her most? When Shane decided to leave this world, he traveled down to Bray in County Wicklow where he must have spent at least some happy days with his mother. Shane's father and the Irish courts removed him from Sinéad's custody with the excuse that she suffered from "depression." Imagine if all courts and fathers tore custody away from all mothers who suffer from depression. Statistics say that one in seven women experience postpartum depression, but I'd guess that number as deliberately, absurdly low.

I do have empathy for Shane's father and can imagine what he might be feeling. Sinéad reached out to him publicly about Shane's death, her message, one of deep love and compassion for his loss. She was extremely loving and fought like a lioness during the custody battles. With Shane, she walked away with a mere token, an allowance of supervised visits.

[3]Sinéad O'Connor, "Tiny Grief Song," *Universal Mother.*

The Bray house was decorated with her children in mind, as well as the lightening of her own spirit—rainbow-colored rooms, soft touches in cozy sofas and pillows, and views of the Irish sea through sun-colored tulips in stained glass. I see Sinéad and Shane napping on the huge bed made for dreaming, under the watchful eye of Lord Vishnu in blue. (Sinéad had a huge mural of Vishnu painted on the wall in a celestial sky of azure as headboard and ceiling in the master bedroom. She was a lover of all sacred paths she did not deem oppressive. On her last recorded LP *I'm Not Bossy, I'm the Boss* is a song called "The Vishnu Room.") After her beloved boy took his own life, did she feel unneeded and abandoned by the others? I imagine her other children loving and admiring her deeply, while keeping a safe distance from their publicly branded "crazy"[4] mother so as not be pulled into the public maelstrom, or into her whirlwind of motherly need and deep sense of loss. Women who refuse to carry the gendered cross have often been pathologized as mentally ill through the ages. As an abuse survivor and an outspoken activist, Sinéad had every reason to be uneasy in this world, hence difficult to be in relationship with for those unaware and disinterested in the systems of harm that create dis-ease[5] for women.

I believe *Universal Mother* was Sinéad's self-healing spell, mandatory care after being repeatedly crucified for telling

---

[4]https://www.nytimes.com/2021/05/18/arts/music/Sinéad-oconnor-rememberings.html.

[5]Etymology of disease, from Old French, desaise, lack of ease. *des-* (expressing reversal) + *aise* "ease."

the truth. Like balms of Gilead, these fourteen songs come to us from the ethers through a voice that shook the world—an Irish woman's voice with a heart-based ganza tongue, where the cerebral oxygen tank of obfuscation shifts toward a deep dive into the womb. Here on the pages, I swim beside her and won't hold back, hyped on the H2O of resistance. In other words, this book smells like *woman*. Rebel girl recalcitrance. It's filled with wom(b)anly textures like blood, guts, viscera, motherhood, and mysticism. It may trigger alternating symptoms of repulsion, love, nausea, guilt, rage, shame, and wonder. Which begs the question: if biologically born men were capable of growing bodies inside themselves, then giving them life, would the gift's extraordinary pain and the awe it inspires make them chill the hell out about women's equality? I doubt it. For one, they'd never be able to bear the physical agony or fathom its selfless power. Although Babylon wouldn't agree, isn't the ability to grow life and to give life from the body the greatest power of all? That power terrifies the patriarchy into continually attempting to force women into subjugation, ruling over our bodies to this very day.

Sinéad begins the text of her CD booklet for *Universal Mother* with excerpts from the pagan/Wiccan prayer, *The Charge of the Goddess*,[6] which indicates her witchhood sans a stitch of remorse. If this book of thoughts on Sinéad and *Universal Mother*, as viewed through the lens of women's ongoing plight on earth, were to elicit new considerations

[6]https://www.learnreligions.com/charge-of-the-goddess-history-and-variations-4151704.

in blinkered hearts around women's oppression, well, that would be grand. I'm prepared to be rejected for my theories and opinions, as she was. And like her, not to give two fucks.

Sinéad O'Connor is the broken, sacredvoice of Mother Ireland. As my occasional spectral roommate, she doesn't like this description. After me presenting the case for it, and she, banging pots and calling it "arrogant shite," I demanded the proclamation as my one mandatory concession, or she'd have to go a'haunting elsewhere. (She loved Curtis Mayfield. His song, "Here but I'm Gone," comes to mind.)

Sinéad repeatedly called out the cruelty of a world that has us racing toward transhumanism and the devastation of Mother Earth and her people. A world immeasurably brutal to Sinéad made her battered heart as gentle as a lamb's, yet she refused to suffer fools and would often strike back at her attackers with the venom of truth. She bathed that same hurtful, punishing world in the warmth of a mother's tenderness with her miraculous voice, words, and melodies. Sometimes she sang with a woman's wrath that only the bravest dare to let loose on the world. She knew what we needed. When she expressed her anger, Sinéad didn't seek retribution. She distilled the pain into a fierce, compassionate revenge. With love, through music.

I like to think that a large part of Sinéad's courage was born when she gave birth to her first child Jake, who makes an appearance on this LP. Jake would have been about five years old when she exposed the Catholic Church's sins on Saturday Night Live (SNL). How courageous she was. Motherhood continued to shape Sinéad through the decades.

She was our Lioness of Judah, Shuhada' Sadaqat, a natural mystic, Mother Bernadette Mary, lover of Rastafari, Islam, spiritualism, Sufism, Judaism, Catholic mysticism, Knights Templar, Kabbalah, Buddhism, and Hinduism.Immortal pursuer of paths to the sacred, appropriation be damned. God is One and we are One All, arriving with a wail through the vulvic tunnel of Sheela na gig.[7]

The word *woman* is under threat of erasure these days. In 2021, the cover of *The Lancet*[8] (the world's highest impact academic medical journal) stated: "Historically, the anatomy and physiology of *bodies with vaginas* have been neglected" [Um, my italics]. Are we supposed to thank you, *Lancet*, for acknowledging how our health has been criminally ignored while you erase our identity in the same blood-soaked sentence? Although she was opposed to labels about her sexuality and refused to be boxed in, Sinéad always identified as a woman and mother, making this clear in interview after interview.

She told Pride Source in 2014:

[7]Sheela na gig: stone carvings of a naked woman flagrantly exposing her vulva. First sitings dating back to 1000–1200 CE, with the largest number occurring in Ireland. See https://www.britannica.com/art/Sheela-Na-Gig.

[8]The September 25th, 2021, cover of the British medical journal, *The Lancet*. After a tsunami of objections, editor-in-chief (white and man, of course) Richard Horton issued a half-hearted apology. The attempt to erase the word "woman" and their identities is ongoing. In June 2023, John Hopkins University defined "lesbian" as "a non-man attracted to non-men" in its glossary of LGBTQ+ terms.

I think if you fall in love with someone, you fall in love with someone, and I don't think it would matter what they were. They could be green, white, and orange, they could be whatever the opposite of gay or straight is. I don't believe in labels of any kind, put it that way. If I fall in love with someone, I wouldn't give a shit if they were a man or a woman.[9]

The Lion and the Cobra was released in October of 1987. In the summer of 1988, Sinéad headlined London Pride alongside Erasure when Pride was a protest; a month before Pride, Margret Thatcher's Section 28 law went into effect, banning local authorities and schools from "promoting" homosexuality. Homophobes always spin dignity and inclusion as "promotion." Sinéad's staunch allyship was an incredible boon to the LGBTQ+ community. In 2017, she donated thirty years of her clothing to trans youth via the Transgender Equality Network Ireland.

In utter humility, she engaged in various volunteer work with causes that grabbed her heart, and she almost never spoke of this work publicly. She personally reached out to people who'd been abused in the "care" system in Ireland and worked with veterans in a US veteran's hospital as a bedside companion to the dying and alone. The war-wounded intrinsically recognize one another and understand the ways of comfort.

I believe Sinéad would have laughed her ass off at an identity politrick pushing to erase the deeply coded, sacred

[9]https://pridesource.com/article/67109–2.

word "woman." Pilloried relentlessly for her causes and actions, imagine if she'd been a lesbian and had a woman partner—pile that on and there would have been no medieval torture device brutal enough to punish. As a recording and performing artist, I have stories of evisceration for daring to be free sexually and out as a queer woman in the late 1980s. Not many women with celebrity status are brave enough to fight the new riptide of misogyny or put boots on the ground for our autonomy, as was implicit in all Sinéad said and sang. Too many brilliant women are petrified of the current tide of cancellation and would never dare disrupt the flow of entitlements they receive for buttoning up their lips. In essence, Sinéad was a witch of great magnitude, burned at the stake again and again. As she grew older and without a wise coven to protect and defend her, I imagine how hard it must have been to face old age alone, with older women diminished and damned as the hag, the crone, the witch beneath the "crazy bitch." The world did her head in. From the depths of her keening, I hear the ancestral mothers and their babies who grew up without role models and mirrors. Sound vibrations reflecting so many caged longings. She screamed, she wailed, she cried for us, whispered to us, lullabied, and honored all our holy ghosts.

Women, especially working-class women, carry rucksacks of intergenerational trauma, and this is certainly true of Irish women. Buried stories of mothers who struggled to survive the genocide of their dreams and their children's dreams, or didn't even see dreaming as a spiritual possibility, breathe through the songs on this LP. Western civilization and parts beyond, held to the absurdity of woman being a rib pulled from man's body when the opposite was the literal truth—man entered this world from the womb of woman. As a working-class Irish woman, Sinéad was a beast of intergenerational trauma's burdens. No matter how much it broke brains and hearts, most women who made it through the wars on women intact through the centuries did so by choosing to ignore pronouns while reading history and fiction. There was a panoptic void of inspiring women's stories. Where boys and men had (and have) an abundance of guideposts on their journeys, the utter despair of the absence of women role models for girls in earlier generations could have proven fatal to the soul in the search for life and meaning.

In the ganza tongue, the word "woman" becomes a Purple Heart, the medal awarded to our soldier brothers wounded or killed on the battlefield. Keep trying to take it away from us and see what happens—an army of valiant goddess fantômes stand behind us, waiting for the cue. May our daughters and granddaughters courageously follow in the footsteps of women warriors like Sinéad, be they noble and quietly potent, or loud and belligerent. Not to fight in whatever way empowers each of us is to face being called "menstruators" or "people with uteruses" instead of women. Diminished, colonized, programmed. We will not become de-sexed machines. Absurd, but true; these moves to erase are really happening. We will never be a gender-fluid society until women are equal. In the words of Angela Davis: "You have to act as if it were possible to radically transform the world. And you have to do it all the time." Sinéad lived by this credo.

There are obvious reasons why women like Marie O'Connor (Sinéad's mother) become monsters or why Sinéad had several nervous breakdowns. (We'll be getting into "Fire on Babylon.") Lately we've developed quite the skill for masking the obvious. It's a skill Sinéad didn't have. She was raw naked truth. In her younger years, she shied away from the feminist label due to seemingly intelligent people (and a generation of young women influenced by the faux-feminism of Madonna and patriarchal women like Camille Paglia) positioning feminists as man-haters—a meme propagated by misogynists of all genders. Later, she dropped the shyness and laid claim to the simple fact that feminism is not about matriarchy, but it's about equality. I'm in accord with Sinéad as a man-loving feminist (which isn't necessarily synonymous with man-sexing feminist). She just whispered to me that if anyone should think man-loving feminist or man-loving lesbian a contradiction, they should "fuck right off."

To the women who might be utterly exhausted but remain prepared to fight on through the oppressions we face, and to the men who honor women and have the guts to speak up and fight for us, this book (and Sinéad's music) is for you. It will take "remembering, then grieving,"[10] sang our Irish illuminator. Let's work together to remove the jackboot of capitalist white male supremacy and its earth-destroying dominations and dance this mess around (thank you, B52s)—in the name of the Mothers, the Brothers, the Holy

---

[10]Sinéad O'Connor, "Famine," *Universal Mother.*

Ghosts, and Sinéad O'Connor. We salute our brave brothers *and* fathers, but only the brave who fight beside us. We lock arms with you.

As Sinéad sings, *John, I love you.*

Clarification: It's true, I do commune with Sinéad's ghost. It's my voice you'll hear on the page, but sometimes, she will insert herself. I've sworn not to utter a word that she wouldn't approve of, lest she smash every plate in the house.

"O, while you live, tell truth and shame the devil!," sayeth William Shakespeare.

(Henry IV)

1
The Tower

I decide tonight is the night.
I know if I do this there'll be war.
But I don't care. I know my Scripture.
Nothing can touch me. I reject the world.

—Sinéad O'Connor[1]

On October 3, 1992, accompanied by a full orchestra, Sinéad is about to present the first of two songs on SNL; a fragile, nearly whispered version of Loretta Lynn's "Success (Has Made a Failure of Our Home)," turned torch song on the singer's tongue. The bold, shaven-headed punk girl will not disappoint; this Irish girl, she knows no shame, but she "do know Mandinka." It's not like she didn't warn the suits of her insubordination straight out of the box.

"Success (Has Made a Failure of Our Home)" is buoyed by a full orchestra, creating dramatic interstitial swells and

[1]Article and interview with Sinéad by Harriet Johnston for the Daily Mail, January 8, 2022 https://www.dailymail.co.uk/femail/article-10381723/How -Sinéad-OConnors-son-struggled-tough-upbringing.html.

breaks between verses and refrains. The orchestra dips to a soft bed of strings as Sinéad lays down the first tender words and notes. She may be singing the story of her own rise to fame and the mess it's made of her personal life. (Her first marriage to John Reynolds, who'll remain her lifelong best friend, writing collaborator, and producer, had dissolved a year earlier in 1991.)

Her graceful neck and collarbone glow nearly translucent, hands fidget shyly, eyes flutter down and back to us with a delicate sadness. The story flows from her eyes as much as from her mouth. A break in the tenderness, a silent pause, then with two smacks of a drum, the orchestra breaks into a sharp swell worthy of a Leonard Bernstein crescendo. Sinéad improvises, the words taking over her body: "I've never changed! I'm still the same!" The desperation, naked now in true punk glory as her voice breaks into an angry keening, "Am I not your girl?" repeating to an abrupt stop. Anyone who has caught their heart at the most formidable performances by Piaf, Garland, and Callas will never doubt they've witnessed something near miraculous. The performance is merely a prelude.

When we return to the concluding moments of SNL, Sinéad returns to a darkened stage and approaches the microphone. The orchestra is gone; she's alone now. Her striking posture is framed by chiaroscuro light. Near her, nine white pillar candles burn, invoking an atmosphere of ritual. Nine, the number of completion. A Star of David, also a Rasta symbol of the Lion of Judah, now stands out against the pale skin of her neck. Tied to the mic stand is a red, green, and gold Rastafarian prayer scarf. Head shaven, gaze solemn and grave, she wears the same long white lace dress from the previous song, a dress indistinguishable from a wedding gown. Unbeknownst to the production staff, to everyone but herself, Sinéad is about to commit hari-kari in the eyes of the world. She'll ignore the rehearsal script in an act that will cement her lifelong vocation as a social justice activist. It is an act of revelation that will backfire spectacularly.

She begins to sing/speak the emphatic words of Bob Marley's song "War." The camera slowly creeps into close-up as she continues, eyes locked on the lens— "...the unhappy regime which holds all of us through child abuse, yeah, subhuman bondage . . . Children! Children! Fight! We have confidence in the victory of good over..." and on the concluding word "evil," she holds up a photograph of Pope John Paul II in front of her face and rips it to pieces. As she throws the fragments toward the camera, she commands us to "Fight the real enemy!" Silence—except for one brave soul in the audience who lets out a timid "bravo!" She removes her earbuds, blows out the candles, and leaves the stage.

Sinéad had slipped the pin off the grenade, shattering the mirage of celebrity for the sake of thousands of children physically, sexually, and psychologically abused by the Roman Catholic Church. We stared into her defiant eyes as she dared the world to see the truth. And the world wasn't ready.

The news drip in Ireland began four years after Sinéad's SNL moment in 1996, with abuse survivor Christine Buckley being the first to speak out on RTÈ Radio about the intense physical abuse she suffered in an orphanage at the hands of the Sisters of Mercy, sparking a cavalcade of women and men sharing their stories of institutional abuse. Ireland's Prime Minister Bertie Ahern made a public apology to the survivors in 1999, with a promise of reparations, many of which never came, with some monies being withdrawn. Very few of the perpetrators were convicted.[2] And the weight of these crimes in the press, committed under cover of the church in Ireland, always shifted predominantly to the nuns in the laundries and baby homes, as opposed to the priests.

In early 2002, *The Boston Globe* published its first reports of sexual abuse of children in the US Catholic Church by priests. And in 2012 a local historian in County Galway, Ireland, discovered the death certificates of 796 babies and toddlers at St. Mary's Mother and Baby Home. The tens (maybe hundreds) of thousands of severe abuse victims across decades and centuries are an indelible scourge on the Catholic Church. Commissions of inquiry, truth commissions, and trials continue in the quest for justice. All of it to date validating Sinéad O'Connor's moment of truth—a moment she paid too dearly for.

At just twenty-four years old, Sinéad O'Connor ascended to the top of the pop charts with "Nothing Compares to You." Her rendition of the Prince-composed song totally eclipsed the Purple One's throwaway recording. Let's face it—despite Prince's envious, malicious fit[3] and his family being the financial beneficiaries from her recording, the

---

[2] https://home.crin.org/issues/sexual-violence/ireland-case-study-clergy-abuse.

[3] From *Rememberings* by Sinéad O'Connor. She recounts how she had to escape Prince's home and his venom. pp. 152–60.

song will always belong to Sinéad alone. There's a backstory here. Prince fired his manager Steve Fargnoli in 1989, and the two were embroiled in a legal battle when Fargnoli began managing Sinéad. There are several versions concerning who suggested Sinéad cover the song, but I'm betting on Steve Fargnoli. He may have guessed that the publishing income Prince would receive from the song, should Sinéad make it a hit, would help ease whatever monies Fargnoli may have owed the Purple One. (Managers often thieve from their artists, and regarding Fargnoli, this is all pure conjecture on my part.) When Elvis Presley recorded "Hound dog" (written by Lieber and Stoller), he never came close to Willie Mae "Big Mama" Thornton's original—clearly a white boy mimicking the absolute power of a formidable black queer female performer. There is no mimicry coming from Sinéad in her presentation of "Nothing Compares to You." The pathos, the rage, and the longing in her voice are pure duende,[4] which is what sent the artist "formerly known as" into fits. Envy was common with Sinéad; journalists, mostly male, as well as major and minor celebrities without an iota of her talent, were abusive to the point of absurdity. By the time Sinéad had hit Number 1 on the charts, she had already courted controversy with her radical truths and stark, exquisite image as the first female rock star sporting the ineffable eyes of an angel and a defiantly shaved head. Exposed she was, and unafraid to be. Yet Sinéad's greatest strength remained

---

[4]Federico García Lorca's Duende essay, https://turf-projects.com/wp
-content/uploads/2017/12/Lorca_Theory-and-Function-of-the-Duende
.pdf.

her miraculous voice. That divine instrument, forged in the fires of child abuse, trauma, and a lifelong quest for mercy, was both sword and shield.

By the time of the SNL performance, she had already experienced the highs and lows of fame. She'd ignited controversy for her brazen attitude and for being the first bald female pop singer to have reached the Valhalla of rock. Her portrait graced the cover of *Rolling Stone* in June of that year. A mere two months later, her music was taken off the air in a US radio boycott after she refused to have the Star-Spangled Banner played before her show in New Jersey. This sent *Ol' Blue Eyes* Frank Sinatra's knickers into a twist, with him announcing how he'd "like to kick her in the ass!" Quoted in *Esquire* magazine in 1991, she responded: "I can't hit this man back, he's like 78 years of age and I'd probably kill him."

Sinéad stood firm against the blowback, refusing to bow to the strictures of fame and the gendered expectations and demands imposed on female singers. She often recalled the criticism coming from men in the music biz, saying she should just "shut up and sing." "Pinch your lips together. How do you sing if you can't open your mouth?" She never stopped singing and speaking truths to the public, using her celebrity as a platform to call out injustice, proving that she was a force to be reckoned with and was willing to sacrifice celebrity on the altar of truth. She repeatedly spoke about not wanting rock stardom and decided to turn her platform into a soapbox, firing spiritual, revolutionary napalm.

In Tarot, the Tower card represents radical change in its most graphic moment of destruction. The Tower can symbolize aspirations built on unsound foundations. The collapse of the Tower via a lightning bolt is akin to Shiva's dancing foot slamming down to destroy, clearing away so that the opposite foot may rise in the dance of creation. (To create anew in 1999, she'd be ordained as a priest at Lourdes, in an effort to bring a message of love and restore her own faith in the church.) Sinéad's SNL act was her Tower moment. She blew up the mirage of stardom, and she did it righteously. Behind that torn curtain of a photo stood a cabal of priests and nuns called to be guardians of a child's innocence, supposed messengers of God's love now exposed as child abusers.

Two weeks later at a tribute concert for Bob Dylan at Madison Square Garden, Sinéad was meant to sing Dylan's "I Believe in You," a deeply reverent song. When she appeared onstage, the crowd of 20,000 plus went ballistic, waves of roaring boos drowning out the cheers. The shock provoked her to launch into a repeat of the Marley song from SNL, with a strong punch on the words "child abuse." Even though she'd showed up to pay tribute to him after being mercilessly crucified by the public, cowardly Dylan hadn't a word of comfort or kindness for her. The only person who came to her aid in that moment was Kris Kristofferson. Concert management asked Kristofferson to get her off the stage, but he wasn't having it. Instead, he approached her onstage with a warm embrace, telling her, "Don't let the bastards get you down." Kristofferson continues to praise her courage.

After these back-to-back public spectacles, a bloodlust of vilification ensued. Across the street from her record label's office in Rockefeller Center, protestors drove a 30-ton steamroller over her cassettes, CDs, and LPs on national television. NBC, SNL's master, banned her from ever performing again on the network. Death threats rained in on Sinéad and her team; celebrities and politicians issued public takedowns. On SNL, Joe Pesci weaved Sinéad-bashing throughout his opening monologue, ending with, "I would have gave her such a smack." I watched an early screening of *Nothing Compares*, the documentary about Sinéad from Irish filmmaker Kathryn Ferguson, and the most outrageously grotesque insult came from a woman—Camille Paglia—a so-called feminist and social critic trending at the time: "In the case of Sinéad O'Connor, child abuse was justified." If only the collective gasp of fifty-plus viewers in the screening room had the power to turn Paglia to dust.

Although Sinéad never boasted about it, justification was righteously hers when the scandal first broke in 2002, fittingly, on the Catholic calendar's Feast of the Epiphany. *The Boston Globe* began publishing a series of reports that the Catholic Church in the United States had been covering up child abuse by priests for decades. The hits kept coming. In 2010, Pope Benedict XVI issued a public apology to the victims of sexual abuse throughout the decades (and most likely, the centuries) by Catholic priests in Ireland. At the time, did anyone write about how Sinéad O'Connor had been vilified for publicly calling out the abuse eighteen years previous? Did anyone shout praises for her bravery? Her prescience? "One poet says of Cassandra that when she stood up to prophecy she shone like a lamp in a bomb shelter."[5]

---

[5] *After Sappho* by Selby Wynn Schwartz, p. 47.

Where were the poets when Sinéad needed them? Why were more brave lamps not set afire?

And yet, what was worse? Sinéad "blaspheming" the church? Or blaspheming the sacred cow of stardom? The appearance of her blowing up her career also cast a glaring light on the hypocrisy of celebrity, of those petrified to speak to social justice causes for fear of losing fans, wealth, and status. No other guest or regular on SNL stood up for her the night she tossed that truth grenade. I want to be able to say that Sinéad gave not one flying fuck. She'd gain back her strength, but for two years after, she couldn't escape death by a thousand cuts. The media was brutal to her. As she predicted on her sophomore record, *I Do Not Want What I Haven't Got*, "These are dangerous days. To say what you feel is to make your own grave."[6]

Sinéad O'Connor was among the first to face the guillotine of cancel culture, and in spectacular fashion. Despite all the public abuse, being ridiculed and labeled as crazy (the usual cliché slapped on outspoken women of courage), she had no regrets. She took the blows, suffered for it, and survived. She was living in America at the time, and her family in Ireland were terrified for her. The public vitriol was so overwhelming that they feared she'd be shot, assassinated.

She moved back to Dublin to recharge, went to a healer for a rebirthing session, and painted the rebirth as a beautiful image for the cover of what would be her next LP, *Universal Mother*. (Her original artwork is "lost," probably in the

---

[6]Sinéad O'Connor, "Black Boys on Mopeds," *I Do Not Want What I Haven't Got*, 1990.

custody of a 1980s art department employee or executive of Chrysalis Records NYC.) She kept her loved ones close and began studying bel canto, a style of operatic singing. Two years after the SNL and Madison Square Garden events, she reemerged with a soul-baring, healing work called *Universal Mother*. No public persecution could sway her from remaining true to herself, nor find her surrendering to the world's hypocrisy.

OH NO

IN THE SUN

MYSELF TO RETRIEVE

AN ELF ARROW THAT SINGS

ONLY TO YOU, CROCODILE BOY

OUTSIDE YOUR MOTHER'S GARDEN

SO LET'S TAKE A LOOK SHALL WE SING

MY LOVE MY LOVE MY LOVE SEEING ME

USE STARS AS LADDERS TEETH SO FAR FROM

PEOPLE'S IDEAS OF STATE WHAT SHE'S BEEN

GUILTY OF BUT THEY DIDN'T KNOW THAT

FACE THE FUTURE

LEAPING WOMEN COULD

LET TEARS FALL LIKE FIRE ON

A CHRISTIAN COUNTRY IRRELEVANT

BABYLON BABYLON BABYLON BABYLON

2
Music as Mother

Indian Sufi master Hazrat Inayat Khan[1] writes that, according to Hindu philosophy, the shortest way to attain spiritual heights is by singing. The three basic kinds of vocal tonal expression are: *jelal*—power, *jemal*—beauty, and *kemal*—wisdom. In turn, five qualities of the voice reveal the character of a person. The earth quality gives hope, encouragement, and is tempting. Water quality is healing, soothing, and uplifting. Fire is arousing, exciting, and can also be horrifying. It is the voice of awakening, as in the Old Testament's tongues of flame or words of warning. Air quality in the voice lifts one away from the earth's plane, and the ether quality is inspiring and healing. Otherworldly: the most intoxicating of all five, "sound being the most potent and effectual magic agent, the first of the keys which opens the door of communication between mortals and immortals."[2]

---

[1] *The Mysticism of Sound and Music* by Hazrat Inayat Khan.
[2] Helena Blavatsky, The Secret Doctrine, Vol. I.

Sinéad intrinsically understood how to use each and how to combine these qualities in her voice. She possessed them all and knew how to leap from the whispered etheric to volcanic firestorm, all in the space of eight bars. Each song was a vessel, its shape dictating which tonal expressions she'd use to inhabit the structure and express the song's story. She was a lover of ragas and mantras. John Reynolds related how she was obsessed with mantras from early on, constantly sending new ones to John and dozens in the few weeks before she died. It makes perfect sense she'd embrace mantras since the power of repetition in chant and song is known to create healing by calming the turbulence of the mind and the nervous system. Sound can literally rearrange the molecular physiology of brain and body.

Like many of the songs on *Universal Mother*, "Thank You for Hearing Me" cycles between two chords in a mantra of gratitude. Hazrat Inayat Khan speaks of the power of illumination resulting from the vibration of certain words repeated—what ancient Sufis called *dhikar* (*zikar*). Chanting and mantras are cross-spiritual exercises and are based on science in that sound waves physically rearrange matter, as the study of cymatics has proven. Sound is now being employed in medicine via acoustic engineering, where heart cells can be configured into healthier patterns via the frequency and amplitude of applied sound vibrations.[3] For Sinéad, I imagine her believing it possible to chant away

---

[3] Article: Sound Research, Scientific innovations harness noise and acoustics for healing by Hanae Armitage https://stanmed.stanford.edu/innovations -helping-harness-sound-acoustics-healing/.

the fear, the cruelty, the ghosts, and the rage. To chant the dysregulation into a finer, more beautiful geometric pattern. If not for a complete banishment, a respite, at least.

Sinéad's voice was sometimes compared to singers like Björk and Alanis Morisette, but aside from the stridency and explosive punch of those voices, her voice was incomparable. It was a distinctly Irish voice. Many of the songs on this LP can be considered ancient types of Irish music, of which there are three distinctives: *geantrai* (celebratory songs), *suantrai* (lullabies), and *goltrai* (lamentations). You won't find songs of celebration here, other than the last—"Thank You for Hearing Me"—a celebration of gratitude. The LP is, for the most part, made of lullabies and lamentations, and even in the aggressive cuts, the profound sense of loss and melancholy leaks through. Sean-nós is the traditional Irish form of singing, and of the variations, the Northern Irish style is the less ornamental. There is a holding of notes for long moments, in the manner of chanting, say, OM, in the Hindu tradition. She doesn't sing in Irish on this LP (I've been warned not to call the Irish language *Gaelic*), but the feel is here in spades. She'll go on to record the LP *Sean-nós Nua* (new old-style) in 2002, an LP of traditional Irish songs, including two songs sung in Irish.

Between her SNL moment and the recording of *Universal Mother*, Sinéad also studied bel canto with the same Dublin teacher, Frank Merriman, who'd once instructed her father. Merriman told her, "I'm not a singing teacher, I'm a freer of voices."[4] And in Sinéad's words, he told her, "If a fire went

---

[4]https://www.irishcentral.com/culture/entertainment/Sinéad-oconnor-now-a-singing-teacher-130907018-237415381.

off in this room, you could scream fire! at the height of any scale. But if you went to sing it, you couldn't. Meaning? The emotions will take you to the notes. The notes are insignificant. The scales are insignificant. The breathing techniques are insignificant. Singing is ALL about emotion. Not notes."[5]

Bel canto, translated as beautiful singing, was originally a style of mid-eighteenth to early nineteenth-century Italian opera. A host of definitions are out there describing bel canto, but common threads are its emphasis on the emotion of the song, on sublime beauty, subtlety and nuance, and the ability to speed up and slow down freely (rubato). There is also the prominence of the voice over the orchestra. Two of the greatest bel canto roles are Lucia of Donizetti's *Lucia di Lammermoor*, and Bellini's *Norma*. I still swoon over Maria Callas singing Norma's bel canto like no other, in my opinion. I'm ignorant about opera but know real blood, real emotion when I hear it. There is blood in Callas's voice, and there is blood in Sinéad's. When I asked John if Sinéad's voice changed after her bel canto lessons, he thought it gave her more strength to hold longer notes. When you're an extraordinary singer and you also train, you move far beyond musical reproach. According to Sinéad, bel canto lessons helped her with confidence, to get out of her own way when feeling insecure about hitting a note, and to distract herself away from the head and into the body's inner chambers.

[5]https://Sinéadoconnor.tumblr.com/post/10765767303/today-in-her-web-site-sin%C3%A9ad-talks-about-singers.

The Hindu/Sufi mystical singing, Sean-nós, and bel canto. I hear several techniques that these three manners of singing have in common—the holding of notes to feel the resonance of vibrations in the body and out into the air, and an emphasis on the expression of deep emotion. The body's ability to use sound as a tool of healing cannot be underestimated, and it's an alchemystical philosophy as ancient as unmarked time.

All three styles of singing connect directly with the vagus nerve as do humming, chanting, and holding long notes.[6] The larynx is connected to the vagus nerve, which is the main nerve in our bodies running from the brain to the stomach. It is the root river from which all nerve tributaries flow throughout the body. The tone of the vagus nerve affects every internal organ and, in terms of sound, can be soothed by singing, gargling loudly, and humming. One study concluded that a short duration of singing improved vascular function acutely.[7] Many studies have been and are being conducted on humans generating sound to stimulate vagal tone, showing that many populations dealing with PTSD, including veterans and sexual assault survivors, benefit greatly from choral singing to playing in drum circles. The communal practice of vagal nerve stimulation through making sound with a group is a destressing exercise that also fosters a sense of community. Making sound, good sound together is an antidote to the epidemics of stress and loneliness in our current world.

[6]https://www.everydayhealth.com/neurology/vagus-nerve/guide/.
[7]https://www.ncbi.nlm.nih.gov/pmc/articles/PMC9339901/.

These free practices are losing a bit of airtime due to new technologies. The vagus nerve stimulator commercial market has come online with a swarm of devices that are basically vibrators with new shapes and patents. These are external hand-held or wrap-around-your-neck devices you apply to specific points on the neck, with different pulses, to stimulate the vagus nerve. Medically approved devices are subcutaneous, which are implanted under the skin and used predominantly in the treatment of epilepsy and depression.

Not to disparage these devices, since they all serve functions in healing and the alleviation of various symptoms in severe cases of dysregulation. I am not a doctor. But I can see clearly how consumer capitalism doesn't want us to depend on our own anatomy to heal ourselves—to know that the music in our cellular makeup is more than capable of stimulating the vagus nerve. *Don't pay attention to the vibrations of notes your body can generate and how they affect your nervous system; this implanted chip in your neck will do it for you!* To think big tech and the medical cabals are not working together is blindness. Social engineering pushes cultural agendas and manufactures desires; it does not cater to public desires that evolve from nowhere. Believing in machines instead of getting to know and work with the power of our own biology is an agenda. Transhumanism in action. As more discoveries come to light about the effect of sound on matter, the ancient cymatics that were spiritually aligned with the science of sound might help us alter the course of this march toward biological disempowerment.

As for the endoscopic view and what the voice looks like in action, have your larynx examined by a camera and watch the monitor as you talk, sing, and hum. I have to say it; the anatomy of the larynx is a dead ringer for an open mouth with an internal vagina.

The epiglottis is shaped like the upper lip, the corniculate cartilage, the bottom lip. Inside these substantial lips is the vestibular fold, and that's where my eyes popped in the ENT office. The vestibular fold, like labia majora in respiration (opening when you make sound) and phonation (closing), is a dead ringer for the vulva vestibule, with its cave-like opening where the trachea resides. Singing and watching this action on the monitor while the camera caught the magic was certainly revelatory; we all have vaginas in our throats. In Sinéad's case, whether she was aware of the internal throat anatomy's appearance or not, I imagine it as the birthing tunnel through which her ghosts would travel.

In nearly every book I've written, Federico García Lorca's theory of the duende[8] turns up. A concept originating in Southern Spain, Lorca's duende is neither a muse nor an angel to the artist, but a mysterious daemon, guardian of the mysteries that sleep inside the body. I see the duende as a mischievous imp that dares you to grant it access to your most secret emotional wounds. To wake and shake them. Only the bravest artists will surrender to the duende, let it wrestle with the wounds to push and pull and play, then to emerge in an alchemical dance that graces the artist's work with a commanding, blood-fueled essence. In Sinéad's case,

---

[8]Federico García Lorca, "Play and Theory of the Duende" (Argentina, 1933). A spirit that only the bravest of artists let inside, with its consciousness of death and the diabolic.

she was all duende. Her songs and her performances were a deciphering of the duende's frightening and illuminating battles.

Drummer John Reynolds is Sinéad's first husband, father of her first child Jake, producer and co-producer of several of Sinéad's LPs, including her debut, *The Lion and the Cobra*. John and Sinéad met when she was sixteen. In *Rememberings*, Sinéad calls John a "musical midwife."[9] He produced *Universal Mother* with her in 1994 and sees it as the healing musical antidote to everything she'd experienced since SNL in 1992. He and Sinéad had broken up in 1991 but remained great friends and co-parents to Jake. They continued to tour together, with John on drums. Both were living in Notting Hill, London, at the time; Sinéad had a house around the corner from John's flat, where he had set up a home recording studio with ProTools and state-of-the-art Telefunken microphones, purchased with the advances for *The Lion and the Cobra*.

John was playing drums with Jah Wobble's Invaders of the Heart at the time, and after an exciting night of extraordinary energy working with Arabic singers on the Wobble sessions, he stopped by Sinéad's to drop off school clothes for Jake. Hyped on the music he'd just played, he asked if she had any songs in the pipeline and if she might be interested in demoing some songs. She told him she'd been writing some stuff. "Great, come around and we'll get it down. You can come around now, if you like," said John. It was about 11:00 p.m.

The story goes that Sinéad and John drove around London for a bit and then went to John's flat. He set up some keyboards to find the right keys and set up microphones in the bathroom (all that tile and porcelain, great acoustics). What happened next was nothing short of a miracle.

Sinéad sang the entirety of *Universal Mother* in John's bathroom. Apart from "Fire on Babylon" and "Scorn Not His Simplicity," she sang every song a cappella without any written lyrics or notes; she had all the songs memorized in her head. John was shocked. They had recorded a lot together previously, but nothing like this. He knew she'd been carrying those songs for years—like pieces of literature. Complex stories spilling out in an autobiographical flow. All the top lines (melodies) were there with no references and no homemade demo tapes. Pure emotive flow. Bel canto.

Many of the vocal performances on these bathroom demos could not be emotionally bested in proper recording studios. What we are hearing is Sinéad singing her stories late that night in John's home studio. A bit later, the vocal for "Fire on Babylon" was also recorded in that bathroom. She and John would try it again at two or three other studios, but the bathroom take could not be topped. John had written and created the music track for "Fire on Babylon" years before. Although the lilt of reggae is absent, you can hear the track's heavy reggae or dark funk influence, bedeviled by a slowed-down version of Miles Davis horn sample from "Dr. Jekyll," itself an apt metaphor for the two faces of the ghost mother haunting every step this record takes. But the Roman

Catholic Church, also known as the Whore of Babylon, is also present in Sinéad's love for Rastafari. Although she often sang between a whisper and a wail, Sinéad knew how to work a microphone for dynamics. Just in case she broke out with a note that would clip and distort the signal, John had set up a second microphone with a -20 dB pad punched in so they'd have the take no matter what. Having been in studios many times with engineers compressing all hell out of my vocals, I was thrilled to hear that John hates compression and limiting when recording vocal performances as much as I do. Maintaining the emotion and texture of the voice is crucial—compress, and the natural dynamics of the voice go flat. He'd rather ride the gain than squish the emotional daylights out of a gorgeous vocal performance.

Often engineers try and remove all a singer's breaths, but these are part of the expressive emotion of the song. John recalls a time when he stepped out of the studio and, when he returned, an engineer had removed all of Sinéad's breaths. John could see the automated faders dipping to zero as she took each breath, faders flying back up when the breath finished. As if the woman didn't breathe while she sang. Lucky for us, John always pushed back on this technique.

When John played the Babylon track for Sinéad, she let loose, recording a story of suffering at the hands of her mother, riding a cathartic groove that blazes into napalm about 4:30 minutes in. She repeats and wails FIRE! in D#5, then catapults up to a G#6 with full guns blazing. Many operatic coloratura sopranos can't hit that note. It's not a pretty sound in Sinéad's throat and isn't meant to be—it's the tongue of flame, a wailing note evoking awe. It is the duende lurking inside the screaming madwoman of Giannina Braschi's ars poetica,[10] evoked by the cruel mother Marie O'Connor. Reynolds says Sinéad's energy was nearly impossible to contain on the mic, but fortunately, he was able to capture the performance.

I wish Michel Gondry had been half as sensitive when directing the music video for this song. His usual Rube Goldberg fetish is on display, with the childhood home morphing and transforming and eventually catching fire, but the video story comes off as clumsy. There's a wacky machine sharpening who-knows-what and way too much visual diddling going on, distracting from the sheer power of the song. The most striking visual poetic has Sinéad reading a book about Jeanne d'Arc and becoming her at the video's end. It is uncanny how many similarities exist between Sinéad and me. Joan of Arc was my heroine as a child, a rare instance of a woman warrior to rouse the spirit (including her natty fifteenth-century armor and sword). That she ended her valiant battles tied to a stake didn't matter to me as a child. It was Jeanne's courage that inspired. Against all odds she fought for God and country and was willing to die for her beliefs.

There is an arresting video of Sinéad and her band performing "Fire on Babylon" on Top of the Pops in 1994.[11] I performed on this show with Jellybean Benitez in 1988, and the musicians and singers mime to playback. A bit of

[10]Giannina Braschi has written an ars poetica featuring the Duende in *Empire of Dreams* (i.e., "Poetry is this screaming Madwoman").

[11]https://www.youtube.com/watch?v=bUdhwJZE7AE.

a drag, but the audience makes up for the lack of onstage sound. Sinéad must have talked the sound techs at TOTP into giving her a live microphone feed, at least for a part of the song toward the end, where she wails FIRE! and her voice eclipses the playback in a volley of rage. 'Tis a thing of beauty.

"Fire on Babylon" is followed by the exquisite ballad in waltz-time, "John, I Love You." Sinéad often mentioned this song as being about and for her brother, John. Although she does place John in the car when Marie crashed, she only hints at what may have happened to him as a young child, never speaking to it directly out of respect. My guess: the song is about two Johns/Seans. The little brother she couldn't protect and the man who stood by her side throughout her life of making music, John Reynolds. I'll wager the closing song, "Thank You for Hearing Me," is about Reynolds as well, except for a verse about philandering Peter Gabriel. "John, I Love You" is one of the most exquisite love songs I've heard to date, about a sacred and sensual love. Inside all that is sensuous in nature, maternal love is sensuous love, for the love of a woman in its deepest expression is a mother's bodily love. A waltz in three, the song has a strong accent on the two, which makes its cadence unusual and enchanting. It sounds like a baroque lullaby—a soothing love song for a boy once abused, here cherished and beloved by the beholder. It's also a call to believe in the enchantment of a world waiting to be discovered outside the cruel mother's garden.

"My Darling Child," "A Perfect Indian," "All Babies," "Scorn Not His Simplicity," and "John, I Love You" are all Baroque-adjacent lullabies, most in lento time cycling back and forth between two chords of arpeggiated piano motifs. Sinéad is known more for playing guitar, but she composed these on piano. John tells me Sinéad recorded the piano on all the lullaby tracks. She played in perfect harmony with what she was singing and was much better on keys than other musicians they'd bring in to play keys on the same parts; she was always instinctually right about music. (Many of her songs are two chords with her singing against a drone. For instance, going back, "Troy" is just two chords. Mantra-like.)[12]

"Tiny Grief Song" is a heartbreaker. Sinéad sings that Marie's burial date (not year) coincided with the birth of her first child, Jake, in the LP's twelfth track. John claims that the recording of the entire LP was emotionally charged more than any other, but it was listening to her sing "Tiny Grief Song" a cappella that moved him most. The song might appear too dark to be considered a lullaby since it is a keen of mourning. But many lullabies are ultra-creepy, some even sounding like murder ballads—"Rock-a-bye Baby," for instance, with its ending of death by cradle-crash.

Baby snatching is another common theme. My paternal Italian grandmother sang me the lullaby "Ninna Nanna Ninna O," which asks, "Whom shall I give this child to? The witch, the black wolf, the white wolf, or nobody at all?" In the original Irish "Fairy Lullaby," a mother is taken by faeries, and her baby is "strange." (These faeries snatched mothers, putting "changelings" in their baby's places.)

A year ago I was snatched forever,
hush-a-by baby, babe not mine,

---

[12]Interview with John Reynolds, January 2024.

---

from my home to the hill where hawthorns quiver,
hush-a-by baby, babe not mine,
shoheen sho, strange baby O!
You're not my own sweet baby O!

The more macabre lullabies could be considered reflections of a mother's postpartum emotions—the overwhelming fear of feeling that twenty-four-hour vigilance won't be enough to keep the fragile baby alive. Many mothers express feeling near psychosis after the infant is born due to sleepless nights, intense fear for the child's safety and their own mental health, physical weakness due to breastfeeding and a fear of psychic cannibalism, of the baby being vampirish, sucking nutrients and the very soul from the mother—issues that mothers hardly speak out loud, yet all feel in degrees across race, class, and country. Beyond the scope of this book, there is much to be said about the extreme challenges of motherhood, the darker aspects of feeling abjection due to "Images of blood, vomit, pus, shit, etc central to our culturally/socially constructed notions of the horrific." Yet "there was a time when a 'fusion between mother and nature' existed; when bodily wastes, while set apart from the body, were not seen as objects of embarrassment and shame."[13]

Dark fantasies of violence directed at children abound in fairy tales. For instance, *Grimm's Fairy Tales* are rife with bloodlust. The huntsman in the original "Snow White" is told to take the seven-year-old into the forest and return with her

[13] *The Monstrous-Feminine: Film, Feminism, Psychoanalysis* by Barbara Creed, p. 13.

lungs and liver. A mother decapitates her stepson for reaching for an apple in *the Juniper Tree*, cooks him, and serves him to her husband, who asks for seconds. "Frau Trude" turns a girl into a piece of wood and burns her. There's *Jack and the Beanstalk*, with the ravenous giant wanting to grind Jack's bones to make his bread. And we have *Hansel and Gretel* where the Witch, sometimes referred to as the Gingerbread Hag, plots to cook and eat the duo. Morbid stories from collections like the Grimms Brothers are foundational to what we know of nursery literature in the West.

Sinéad's first child Jake's little tune "Am I Human?" is precious. Jake's father John told me how this came about—John would bring him to the studio, strap a pair of headphones on him, and let him perform on the microphone. When Jake heard his voice made otherworldly by effects like reverb and echo, his response was "Am I Human?"—an affirmation of life in contrast to the ghosts of Ireland's Tuam babies, who were hardly treated as human. She follows his voice with an immaculately tender lullaby of love written for Jake, "My Darling Child."[14]

On "Red Football" Sinéad once again summons her mother, recalling being "kicked around the garden." As recounted in *Rememberings*, the cruelty of her mother saying she wanted to "burst her womb" rises as Sinéad slows down her cadence on the line, "my womb is not a football for you." The song also lays claim to her own fragility, the trap of fame appearing in the metaphor of a crocodile encaged in glass in the Dublin Zoo, being tortured by spectators. The end

---

[14]The story of the Tuam babies appears in Chapter 4.

of the song features a chorus of childlike voices singing "la las" in place of "nyah nyahs," a familiar children's payback taunt popular in Britain and the United States that basically translates as "ha ha, I got you back!."

Sinéad wreaks her compassionate revenge in songs. "Scorn Not His Simplicity" is a song written by Phil Coulter, a well-known Irish musician, songwriter, and producer from Derry, Northern Ireland, and a credited producer on the LP. The song is about Coulter's son, who was born with Down's syndrome. It was not intended for this LP, which Sinéad meant to be purely autobiographical to her experience, but because the song is an empathetic story of a disabled child, a story one never really hears in music, she felt it matched the LP's themes. John tells me the song was an afterthought. He'd left the studio for a bit, and when he returned, she and Coulter had already recorded it.

In "All Babies" I hear the rubric for *Universal Mother*:

She hears their calls,
She is mother and father
All babies are crying
For no one remembers God's name.

The ghosts of Ireland's lost from the Magdalene laundries and the Mother and Baby Homes reach out to us once again in this song. Following the line about God's name, Sinéad keens. It's a wail of loss for the forgotten God in us all, the epicene God that man rejects in favor of his own omnipotence, his domination over woman and earth. Sinéad's is the sorrowful wail of our Universal Mother. "There's only love in this world," she sings.

A
GOD
EXPECTS
CHOKING
ON THE ASHES
OF HER ENEMY
YOU GAVE LIFE TO ME
FEEBLE I WAS THEN ME
LITTLE
WOLF
EASILY
AMUSED
NOW
I'M
GROWN
AND
WOMEN
ARE BURIED
AS
A
RACE
FUNDAMENTALLY
PATRIARCHAL
THAT
GOT
ITSELF
BASHED
IN
THE
FACE

3
The Cruel Mother

Ireland created my mother.
The system here created my mother.
And I've come to realize she was a monster.

—Sinéad O'Connor[1]

I begin with a question. Do pregnant mothers fear the possibility of bringing a monster into the world? A vampire child that will eat their souls of any future possibilities? And does that make the mother the monster for feeling these fears? Barbara Creed's *Monstrous-Feminine* examines the idea of women as victims in horror films by flipping the script via a feminist lens, where the monstrous is, in fact, the female reproductive body. I imagine Sinéad's mother, Marie, watching her little girl grow, little Sinéad's mystical eyes hinting at wondrous worlds to come, striking fear into Marie and pre-shadowing a future Marie might never grasp. The child as uncontainable desire, a bud in its tender unfolding,

[1] https://www.rocksbackpages.com/Library/Article/Sinéad-oconnor.

and the monster here was the mother, whose envy wanted to crush the pure, unblemished horror of beauty's future. Marie was the archetype of the envious mother, blaming and punishing her children for the loss of their father's love.

A statement from a recording by Germaine Greer opens the door to *Universal Mother*:

> I do think that women could make politics irrelevant by a spontaneous cooperative action the like of which we have never seen which is so far from people's ideas of state structure and viable social structure that seems to them like total anarchy and what it really is is very subtle forms of interrelation which do not following a hierarchical pattern which is fundamentally patriarchal—the opposite to patriarchy is not matriarchy, but fraternity, and I think it's women who are going to have to break the spiral of power and find the trick of cooperation.[2]

We need a new word for the concept of fraternity.

An escape from the language that does not serve women is a step toward breaking that spiral of power, and O'Connor's musical language is such an exodus precisely because she refuses to hide her deepest emotions. Feelings of matricide hardly show up in the throats of women in pop music. The entire LP is a Wharton's jelly[3] of truths hardly ever spoken

---

[2] Sinéad O'Connor, "Germaine," *Universal Mother*, track #1, taken from a Germaine Greer recording made in 1970.

[3] Wharton's jelly—the gelatinous substance inside the umbilical cord that cushions and supports umbilical vessels. It expresses stem cell genes, most importantly telomerase, and is obtained from the cord after birth to be used

aloud. Out of the gate with the mother assassination of "Fire on Babylon," Sinéad is signaling her refusal to play by the rules. It's a double-whammy of an opening salvo, signaling she will not compromise, daring to be all woman in the highest sense of our sacred codings—as mother, daughter, high priestess, abused child and country, life-giver, and destroyer. In her voice, I hear the desire to escape punishment for being true to the essence of womanhood and dignity, to shake off a contrition society insidiously and sometimes overtly expects from us.

Many rock critics (men and women alike) ripped *Universal Mother* for its emotional witnessing, calling it therapy as music. (Flip it. If it weren't for music *as* therapy, where would any of us be?) I came across a review by a woman critic so disturbed by the record's vulnerability and pathos, of what she refers to (and I paraphrase) as O'Connor's swings between pomposity and pain, humbleness and self-effacement, that she concludes her piece by scolding O'Connor, telling her to stop trying to save the souls of the world and to save her own. The review is an ignorant stab at disguising the critic's fear of her own shadow. When facing the mirror, internalized misogyny shudders and turns away. Attacking other women is an easier, more welcome path than confronting the men responsible for the system that hurts women, the latter a path often resulting in sackcloth and ashes as it did when Sinéad called out il Papo—Pope John Paul II—and the men of the

in stem cell therapies and regenerative medicines. As an after-birth tissue, it is normally discarded after every birth, presenting ample opportunity for harvest.

Roman Catholic Church for covering up their worldwide shuffle of unpriestly pedophiles.

Sinéad uses word and note as a healing wand and weapon on this LP. By exposing herself, she creates a portal for the unafraid—pass through and meet the sorrowful mother in us all. After what she'd survived in previous years—the childhood abuse, the SNL tower moment, the Dylan concert where she was shamed off the stageand so on—recording this LP feels like her alchemical attempt to transform the pain with music. By doing so, she will help to calm the anxieties of hurt women *and* men who are secretly terrified at the idea of annihilation by a threatening mother. Look at the Cruel Mother, she tells us, with naked eyes and heart, so as never to become her, and bathe in the warmth of the good mother's voice. Sinéad's vocation was forged in the fires of an unholy childhood of abuse and a lifelong search for comfort and mercy.

One of Sinéad's epic crushes, Peter Gabriel, could write and record expository songs like "Digging in the Dirt" and "Mercy Street" but not be ripped for it. Of course. As beautiful as "Mercy Street" is (a salute to Anne Sexton), Sinéad's songs here go deeper into a woman's psyche by disrobing from stylistic maneuvers. She wants to pierce the heart of stark truths, drilling down into the sweet and sometimes bitter core, excavating hurts that many women feel obligated to remain silent about in the attitude of "go along, in order to get along." Only the brave dig into the dirt of their own souls in the context of this strange world we live in and how we allow it to shape and/or distort us, depending on our choices. By bringing up what they courageously find, some artists will expose the discoveries in their work with a raw generosity, inviting us to open to our shadow selves. Sinéad is unafraid of what most think of as a horror show. In the words of Jean Genet, Sinéad understands that "To escape from horror, bury yourself in it."[4] Within many of the songs is a tender understanding of the corruption seeded by a society that turned her mother, turns many women and men, into monsters. At the LP's denouement, she'll have weeded out the cruelty with rage and extreme compassion, emerging with gratitude as the kind mother and protectress of an empirical wisdom that only the open-hearted might be warmed by.

Hélène Cixous once defended her own writing as poetically political, politically poetic. In an interview with Verena Andermatt Conley, Cixous stresses the poetic over the political that represses, a politic that is "cruel and hard and so rigorously real that sometimes I feel like consoling myself by crying and shedding poetic tears."[5] *Universal Mother* is an exploration of this mode of making. Sinéad is poetically political (and vice versa) throughout this LP. "Fire on Babylon" is the most aggressive and most violent track on the record, justifiably so. It was necessary for her to come out hard with a beat-back to child abuse at the hands of her mother, and for those who've experienced child abuse, we too console ourselves and live our anger vicariously through her keening. She will open this autobiographical LP with her banishment of the Cruel Mother and Babylon and will

---

[4]From *Our Lady of the Flowers* by Jean Genet.
[5]*Hélène Cixous: Writing the Feminine* by Verena Andermatt Conley, Appendix, p. 139.

begin the LP's closure with a song about Mother Ireland, a mother country colonized, abused. The very last song on the LP, "Thank You for Hearing Me" is a mantra of gratitude for having been given the space to be heard, in private and on the worldwide stage. She sheds elegiac tears over every track on this LP—tears of rage and loss, of tenderness and care, and of longing. In Portuguese, some will say she sings *saudade*.[6] Of being on this earth, but not of it.

Child abuse is a bird with a broken wing caught in the throat. When we allow the bird to sing its truth, it can be thrashed into silence and shame, as proven by what happened to Sinéad after exposing the church's crimes against innocence. That she dared to speak about familial secrets damaged many of her closer relationships. Familial sexual abuse and violence usually remains buried six feet under; truths too scalding to the touch. . The truth remains: Sinéad O'Connor was physically and sexually abused by her mother. No one wants to hear/see/speak of this kind of evil yet so many of us know it—if not from firsthand experience, near enough. Without air, wounds fester.

I have been close to several women whose fathers made them into their child-lovers when they were little girls. I have borne witness to what is left behind in place of the active abuse—an overwhelming fear of hurting daddy, in micro and macrocosm, narcissism,, and a reliance on sexual desire from others and sexual release as a stand-in

---

[6]*Saudade*—a Portuguese word that nearly defies translation—speaks of a melancholic longing for a beloved elusive presence, one that may never even have been something, or someone, yet resides in the marrow of our bones.

for love and self-esteem. Fathers sexually assaulted these girls, sometimes when they were as young as four years old, on a regular basis. Too young to know the difference between wrong and right, old enough to know they were being touched in a forbidden, dangerous way, while also trying to fathom the wrongness and being physically hurt by their main protector. The disgust I feel over this perversion of innocence makes it hard to detangle feelings into words; how the rot of sexual childhood abuse is nigh impossible for many to eradicate creates a heavy sorrow. Like a decaying tooth that will not budge from gums calcified by the terror of shame and patriarchal retribution, it is a rot that only the bravest dare to investigate in both a personal and cultural context. And it's always the survivor's task to do the dirty work, since the sexual killers of young souls never come clean.

To feel weak and lost amidst the cultural ideology of what a real man should be in an über-capitalist society can turn a man to cruelty. Patriarchy hurts and punishes men as well as women, yet men hardly ever use the word, thinking it a feminist battle cry and ignoring how patriarchy is the basis for a sociopolitical system of capitalism that informs and cages their own identity. Cruelty grows from cowardice. Father figure and boss in the home but not in the world, men who commit sex crimes on their own children prey on a child's innocence, believing they'll never be caught or punished for their extreme brand of sadism—not even by wives who too often look the other way. If a man feels he hasn't any outlets to give expression to his imagination, if his curiosity is thwarted by a society that dismisses creativity as the foundational core of life, the sexual energy/spark of creativity can turn into a will to destroy, to use sex as a weapon of power. It doesn't matter if the victim is his own young child. He created them from seed, didn't he? And he can twist and destroy them just as well, in the name of the father.

But what of the mother who abuses her children, sexually, mentally, and physically? What makes such a monster, and what cultural iron maiden confines and shapes her cruelty? In describing the codes of *Universal Mother*, I'll work to unleash the trembling bird within the throat of woman, in Sinéad's name—the shameful truth that women are abusers too, and the reasons they might become so.

Cruelty in human nature is far more complex than man = enemy, woman = victim. All of us, men, women, and third sex alike, struggle within the bars of assorted cultural and gendered cages. There is an ingenuousness around the idea of "men as perpetual perpetrators, women as the perpetual victims, and male sexual violence as the root of all injustice."[7] Generally speaking, when men feel impotent in society, they tend to transform their frustrations into aggression and violence against others, whereas women turn their violence inward to self-harm, hurting their children, and often hurting other women. Mothers abusing daughters psychologically, emotionally, physically, and/or sexually fly under the radar often, and woman as oppressor is a subject riddled with thorns in feminist circles. Yet this woman-on-woman cruelty speaks to the very pulse of why women still do

[7]Maggie Nelson quoting Barbara Ehrenreich, from *The Art of Cruelty* (W.W. Norton & Co. Inc., 2011), p. 68.

not have equal rights. If we refuse to name and articulate this disease of women's inhumanity to women, we will continue our sleepwalk into the divisions patriarchal systems are hard at work maintaining for their dominance.

Sinéad's mother abused her terribly when she was a little girl. She recounts the physical and sexual abuse in her memoir and interviews, hinting at Marie's mistreatment of her brother as well in a lyric from "Fire on Babylon." Marie is all over this record—for instance, kicking Sinéad around the garden in the song "Red Football." Marie's abuse included forcing young Sinéad to lie on the floor naked while she threw cereal and coffee grounds on her body, stomping on her womb, and beating her genitals with a broom. Female sadism toward a child never appears uglier than this.[8]

When Sinéad's father left Marie (and he may have left because of her erratic and possibly dangerous behavior), Marie took out her despair and anger on her children. She initially had custody of the children, and despite whatever financial arrangements were made in the divorce, she decided that she had to steal anything that wasn't nailed down, including alms from the church basket. Marie tutored young Sinéad in the art of thievery, the least of the abuse. Her mother's sadism caused lifelong complex PTSD for Sinéad, who never quite recovered from emotional triggers that can set off cataclysms of unwarranted paranoia and rage. Imagine having PTSD of that nature and suddenly becoming famous,

---

[8] *Rememberings* by Sinéad O'Connor, pp. 28, 31.

where everyone wants a piece of you (and hardly ever the giver they be).

Sinéad calls out the horror of the abusive mother in "Fire on Babylon," exposing Marie as torturer, hinting of what Marie may have done to her brother John. Marie's abuse of her children gives rise to the myth of Euryipedes' Medea, priestess of the goddess Hecate and one of the most frightful women in the Greek pantheon. As she ages, Medea is spurned by her husband Jason, who abandons her and marries a younger woman, Glauce. Medea enacts her revenge on Glauce by sending her an exquisite gown and wreath as a wedding gift. Delighted at the sight of the gifts, Glauce puts on the gown and wreath. Both have been soaked in poison. The wreath bursts into flame and so does the dress, sticking to Glauce's skin and burning her alive. When Glauce's father the King, tries to save Glauce, he too perishes in the fire. Revenge is a gift served hot and not enough of a meal for Medea. "...a mother's heart floods with a mother's horror at what I am not about to do."[9] She proceeds to kill Jason's (and her) two sons.

Marie O'Connor had ongoing mental health problems and was known to be violent. One version of her penchant for self-inflicted car crashes harkens back to a Medea story. Marie nearly killed young Sinéad and herself when Sinéad's older brother ran away. She had vowed to hurt Sinéad in a car accident if her brother didn't return home, and when

---

[9]From *Medea* by Euripides, *World Mythology, An Anthology of the Great Myths and Epics,* Donna Rosenberg (NTC/Contemporary Publishing Group, Inc. 1999) (source).

he refused, Marie drove off and smashed into another car coming from the opposite direction. Neither Marie nor Sinéad was hurt. In *Rememberings*, Sinéad says Marie was driving to mass at Saint Anne's, Dublin, when her car skidded on black ice, colliding with a bus. Her brother John and an unknown man were in the vehicle and survived unharmed.

In all of Sinéad's various descriptions, Marie comes off as the mother from Hell. And yet, she loved Marie madly. There's a chapter in her memoir about her mother's record collection, with discs spanning a wide spectrum—from Johnny Cash and Dusty Springfield to the Irish tenor John McCormack.[10] The music must have represented the benevolent side of Marie, the essence Sinéad loved most about her mother and carried with her as a lifeboat of love.

What is true and what is shielding story? It doesn't matter. Sinéad owes us nothing in her confessions, and it's perfectly reasonable that she'd want to protect family members and her own privacy. She has exposed her pain in ways that most people, especially celebrities, would never admit to. "Fire on Babylon" lays out the torment and the rage of having been a victim of the Cruel Mother. It is a hellfire operatic payback, with a wrath that the goddess Hecate[11] herself would rain down on Medea for her acts of filicide.

"Fire on Babylon" is followed by the exquisite ballad in waltz-time, "John, I Love You." Sinéad often mentioned this

---

[10]*Rememberings* by Sinéad O'Connor, p. 41.

[11]Hecate/Hekate, Greek goddess of the underworld, witchcraft, the night, moon, ghosts, and necromancy.

song as being for her brother John. Although she does place John in the car when Marie crashed, she only hints at what may have happened to him as a young child, never speaking about it directly out of respect.

You'd think Sinéad's astonishing performances of "Fire on Babylon" and "John, I Love You" would vanquish the Cruel Mother once and for all, but the haunting would continue throughout Sinéad's music and life.

Sinéad sings that Marie's burial date (not year) coincided with the birth of her first child in the LP's twelfth track, "Tiny Grief Song." I believe a child's heart maintains a ghostly umbilical cord to the mother's heart—a silver thread of love. Or can it turn dark, a cord that can wrap and choke? Sinéad forever mourned the loss of her mother despite the cruelty she endured at her hands. Yes, it is achingly probable that a child's love for an abusive mother can sometimes surpass the love for a kind mother, because the child is left with a profound sense of longing.

I suffered abuse and abandonment at the hands of my own schizophrenic mother when young. As much as I hated her for it, I understand how the love, especially when a mother passes, can overwhelm the blame. It is a double loss, a twinning heartache.

The heart. If Sinéad's most tender muscle finally gave up, it makes perfect sense. She smoked like a chimney in winter, talked about the day of her mother's funeral and how she wanted to smoke herself to death. She understood how to mask her grief.[12] Healers tell us the lungs are the seat of loss, and

---

[12]*Rememberings* by Sinéad O'Connor, p. 68.

smoke camouflages their mercy-seated residents. That same addiction smothers the heart slowly. To the smokescreen, add a plethora of psychiatric drugs prescribed over many years to treat any number of "diagnosed" mental illnesses: depression, insomnia, narcissism, bipolar disorder, borderline personality disorder, and so on. Her varied diagnoses by an army of psychiatrists and quack carnival barkers like Dr. Phil ran the gamut. Witnessing her very public breakdowns, Sinéad survived longer than many assumed she would. When asked what she was thinking when she literally cried tears in the iconic video of "Nothing Compares to You," she said she was thinking about Marie. That she'd never stop crying for her mother.[13]

And so, what of Sinéad's mother, Marie O'Connor, born Johanna? If we are all deeply influenced by our parents, our lineage and ancestry, Marie's mother and Sinéad's grandmother, Kitty O'Grady, must have carried her own trauma, but not much is known. For some perspective, in 1933 Ireland banned married women from working, and this ban was not lifted until 1973. Sinéad was born in 1966. Women were legally bound into marriage and childbearing if they wanted to feel safe and were forbidden to have careers. If you were obstreperous and did not follow the state-and-church-sanctified trajectory, you'd likely end up in a cage of another kind run by the Irish state conspiring with the Roman Catholic Church. Up until 1996, if a young woman or

---

[13]https://www.dailymail.co.uk/tvshowbiz/article-12343355/Sinéad -OConnor-revealed-iconic-Compares-2-U-tears-abusive-torturous-mum -never-stopped-crying-over.html.

teenage girl dared to show sexual agency, became pregnant out of wedlock, defied her parents, committed truancy or petty thievery, ran away from home like Sinéad, or indulged in any behavior not deemed to be correctly feminine, off to a Magdalene laundry she'd go. These "homes" forced girls and women into slave labor. If pregnant, your baby might end up buried in an unmarked grave or sold to the highest bidder.

That Sinéad found solace and inspiration in one of these homes did not surprise me. I too felt safety in such a place. And yet, as did I, the darkness she'd eventually discover there would cast an evil shadow over any sense of safe harbor felt.

HER

RED CHEEK

RAYS ON THE WEATHER

I'M NO ANIMAL SO LIFT MY HEART

THANK THE ACHING BLACK ANGELS

THROUGH DEATHS ON LAND ON SHIPS

SAILING THIS TERRIBLE OCEAN KNOW THAT

IT'S NOT PERMANENT ME LITTLE STREET FIGHTER SO

IF YOU LOOK NOW THEN YOU'LL SEE THE WHY OF

MY GRIEF MY GRIEF MY GRIEF MY GRIEF MY GRIEF

WON'T ASK FOR YOUR PITY. THE HOUSE IS

BURNED. BREAK THIS SPIRAL OF POWER

ON A TABLE IN HER YELLOW DRESS

THANK YOU FOR HEARING ME

MOST CHILDLIKE

YOU WERE BORN

MY NINJA

LOVE

4

Hauntings

Because nobody ever gave a shit
about the children of Ireland.

—Sinéad O'Connor, Rememberings

Most of the songs on *Universal Mother* speak to the sacredness of children: "John, I Love You," "My Darling Child," "All Babies," "Scorn Not His Simplicity," "A Perfect Indian," and "Tiny Grief Song."

This is the chapter where you will need to buckle up. Like Sinéad, Irish ancestral trauma on the maternal side is a lineage I carry into this book. The striking similarities between Sinéad and myself have demanded, as part of my vocation here, that I honor her Magdalene story. I spent a year and a half at a Magdalene laundry in Ohio, and Sinéad did time in a Magdalene laundry in Drumcondra when she was a teenager. There was laundry service on the Ohio convent grounds where some of the girls worked unpaid, laundering linens for nearby community businesses, the same as it was in Ireland. Forced unpaid labor (slavery) and the selling of babies were de rigueur in the Magdalene laundries and the Mother and Baby Homes of Ireland. For too many decades, an Irish Catholic "etiquette" of silence hid an architecture of containment for women and girls. Sinéad was sent by her father to live among the nuns in the Magdalene reformatory in Drumcondra, Dublin, when she was fourteen for repeatedly running away from home, petty thievery, and truancy. In the United States, they'd have called her incorrigible, as I was legally branded at thirteen when sent to the Marycrest School for Wayward Girls, run by the Sisters of the Good Shepherd in Independence, Ohio. Sinéad spent a year and a half inside the walls of An Grianán[1] with the Sisters of Our Lady of Charity.[2] Believing in the order's benevolence, her father actually paid An Grianán to "reform" her. In a discussion of *Universal Mother*, I'll skate

---

[1]An Grianán, recently referred to as a "training center" for young women, was originally called High Park Reformatory. The training centers for women and girls were asylums, sanatoriums, and borstals. An Grianán was a girl's jail run by the Sisters of Our Lady of Charity, one of four religious orders in charge of Ireland's many Magdalen laundries. Founded in 1856, An Grianán was the last of the convent laundries to close its doors in 1994. Its fraught history includes restorative justice issues around restitution for forced labor, with cases currently waiting to be resolved.

[2]Interesting twist: On June 27, 2014, after a 179-year split, the Sisters of Our Lady of Charity, founded by John Eudes, merged with the *Good Shepherd Sisters*, founded by Mary Euphrasia Pelletier, to form the Congregation of Our Lady of Charity of the Good Shepherd. Also, https://www.newadvent.org/cathen/06647c.htm.

---

the outer rim of the Magdalene laundries' history vortex or otherwise drown us all in a particularly gruesome Catholic horror show. I'm including this due to these institutions being places of refuge for Sinéad (and myself), albeit briefly, understanding how the consolation of the church's loving mother figures held a promise of care for abused children. And because I hear the ghosts of Ireland's traumatized mothers and babies pulsing through the bedrock of songs on this LP.

The generational trauma of ghost mothers and their children must haunt many Irish women as a dark, spectral memory in the cells. When I visited Dublin in 2023, my breath was seized by a show at the National Museum of Ireland at Collins Barracks by Irish artist Alison Lowry. In *(A)Dressing Our Hidden Truths*, Lowry shows works in glass in an exhibition addressing the crimes of the Mother and Baby Homes and the laundries. Exquisitely rendered and painful to behold, tiny christening dresses for babies made of sand-cast *pâte de verre* (paste of glass) are suspended from the ceiling, lit dramatically. The names of the dead babies and their supposed cause of death are chalked onto the ridges of a washboard. Giant scissors made of glass hang suspended by glass rosaries over mounds of hair. The beauty and horror of these objects magnifies the horrors of 200 years of crimes perpetrated on children and women by the Catholic Church and the Irish state. The scissors and hair enclosed in their glass vitrine feature a quote from the Bible, Old Testament, book of Isaiah, 3:24: "Instead of the Fragrance There Will Be Stench; Instead of a Sash, a Rope; Instead of Well-Dressed Hair, *Baldness* (my italics); Instead of Fine Clothing,

Sackcloth; Instead of Beauty, Branding." This, dripping with evil—the damnation of women by the original patriarchs.

And yet, in different circumstances, timelines, and countries, Sinéad and I both experienced the care and nurturance of at least one nun who tricked us into believing we'd landed in safe harbor away from the cruel mother—that is, until we came face to face with the darkness these institutions tried to conceal. From 1922 to 1998 in Ireland, 81,000 unwed mothers were jailed in 44 Mother and Baby Homes. During that time, over 9,000 children died or disappeared from these homes, most without burial records.[3] While at An Grianán,[4] Sinéad witnessed an infant being forcibly taken from the arms of its teenage mother. An Grianán—translation: in early Irish, a sunny place. A place with a view. A view now unmasked to expose cruelty against babies and women. Many of the healthy babies from these institutions were adopted out, with at least 2,000 of them reportedly trafficked to the United States.[5] After what she'd been through with her own mother, Sinéad must have been deeply affected by witnessing this act of a nun pulling a baby away from its mother's arms. I imagine her vowing to never dream of being cruel to a child. She'd be a good mother, the opposite of all she'd experienced around mothering in her young life. She did not understand how postpartum

---

[3]The Missing Children, documentary https://www.youtube.com/watch?v =0L_AYd3fiSI&t=2926s.

[4]*Rememberings* by Sinéad O'Connor, p. 57.

[5]https://www.irishpost.com/news/heartbreaking-report-reveals-2000-irish -children-sold-us-adoption-mother-baby-homes-160891.

---

might affect her, but then again, does the medical industry understand it, and do they care to?

According to my Irish friends, everyone there heard the whispers about abuse in the Magdalene laundries and the Mother and Baby Homes, yet a conspiracy of silence reigned. I find this fascinating; when signing up and pledging vows to Jesus and an order, nuns in charge of these institutions may not have understood that a form of mothering would be their role. Most nuns may have had no idea what was in store for them since each diocese places you where they wish. For the women and babies in their care, they'd be required to provide a surrogacy not in vitro but by proxy. If nuns were women who wanted children, they'd never have taken vows of celibacy. Yet these were the very women the church anointed as caregivers to discarded, indigent, and forsaken girls and women and their infants.

The bodies of babies younger than one year old were discovered in a mass grave in Tuam, Ireland, on the grounds of St. Mary's Mother and Baby Home, run by the Bon Secours Sisters, an order originating in France. Baby remains were excavated from a disused septic tank.[6] Many of the deaths were logged as flu, whooping cough, measles, and gastroenteritis, pointing to the babies dying from lack of care or starvation, since these illnesses were all treatable. Maybe the nuns thought there were just too many of them to care for and keep alive, and they didn't want the mothers breastfeeding—in other words, bonding. The pretty, healthy

[6]The Secret Mass Graves for Children in Tuam. https://www.youtube.com/watch?v=7RJK8eR9IzM.

babies were sold off to the highest bidders. When the remains were discovered at Tuam in what any moral human would call a horrific case of mass "negligent" homicide, the state was shocked. The church was shocked. (The local diocese and government were not shocked enough to investigate the causes of death for these babies, logged in the hundreds.) A local woman investigated, and Emer O'Toole, writing for the *Guardian*, stated when her research "found death certificates for 796 children at the home between 1925 and 1961 but burial records for only two, it was clear that hundreds of bodies existed somewhere." Nuns at institutions and schools in Ireland were renowned for keeping precise notes and logs. O'Toole continues: "They did not, after all, ascend into heaven like the virgin mother."[7]

Sinéad didn't need the Tuam discovery of 2017 to know what was happening. Most official exposés in Ireland and the United States came much later than her SNL moment. When I spoke with several Irish friends and acquaintances about this issue, everyone knew what was going on but felt helpless due to the state and the church's covert contract of absolute power. Complaints and outrage were met with disbelief and stonewalling. Sinéad recalls reading little articles buried in the back pages of Irish newspapers recounting stories about children abused by priests, stories alleged and never

[7]https://www.theguardian.com/commentisfree/2017/mar/07/catholic-church-children-buried-at-tuam-ireland.
The Catholic Church is shocked at the hundreds of children buried at Tuam. Really? written by Emer O'Toole.

believed.[8] She knew it was this macabre culture genuflecting as pious that polluted the soul of her country and of her own mother.

Sinéad's mother, Marie, kept a photo of Pope John Paul II prominently displayed on her bedroom wall in Sinéad's childhood home.[9] It would be the same photograph she'd carry with her and eventually tear apart on the world stage. Her revolutionary act was profoundly vindicated. Did anyone publicly defend her in 2002 after the Boston Globe's exposé of rampant child abuse by the Catholic Church? In 2017, when the remains of Tuam's dead babies became news, were there any adjacent articles praising Sinéad and connecting the dots of her prescient televised act twenty-five years earlier? Not that I could find. Not until after her death. Shoot the messenger, done and dusted, "For no man delights in the bearer of bad news."[10]

After independence from England in 1937, the Irish state quietly conspired with the Roman Catholic Church to incarcerate poor, marginalized women, many forced into unpaid labor as laundresses, and to traffic their babies. Deeply Catholic Ireland wanted to uphold itself as morally superior to their colonizer England, meaning shameful, unwed pregnant women had to be hidden away. Contraception was not legalized until 1979 in Ireland, prescribed only for legal marriages and family planning

---

[8]*Rememberings* by Sinéad O'Connor, p. 176.

[9]*Rememberings* by Sinéad O'Connor, p. 176.

[10]From *Antigone*, Sophocles.

purposes. That is, contraceptives were only available to married couples.[11] The streets were swept of unwed mothers, promiscuous (or even flirtatious) teenage girls, rebellious girls, runaways, truants, thieves, and prostitutes, of course. In fact, any female deemed immoral by Irish families and/or society could be shipped off to a Magdalene laundry or, when pregnant, to one of the eighteen Mother and Baby Homes in Ireland. Initially created from a need to develop and maintain a patriarchal social and moral order, these institutions also profited well from the enforced free labor of the "fallen" women and girls incarcerated. It didn't matter if a girl was raped, impregnated by a family member, or covered in cigarette burns and bruises—off she'd go to one of these institutions while the perpetrator remained free, the crime unspoken in the family or community. A girl or woman could end up locked away permanently, and the inflicting butcher's crimes never considered. Divorce was not legal in Ireland until 1996, and there were no laws to protect women and their children from abusive husbands. Where were the men, the good fathers, to protect these young women and their babies? Where were the wives and mothers of these pregnant girls sent to prisons? Where were the authorities? When asked these questions in a public talk in Ireland, Irish

[11] https://www.ncbi.nlm.nih.gov/pmc/articles/PMC7120263/#:~:text =Contraception%20was%20not%20legalised%20until,only%20available %20to%20married%20couples.

civil rights leader and former politician Bernadette Devlin paused, then replied: "*Where was God?*"[12]

The remains of 155 women were exhumed from the grounds of the very Magdalene laundry where Sinéad was incarcerated. Some were named, others anonymous. When tombstones pockmarked the courtyards of these institutions, the graves were often identified as "Magdalen of Lourdes" or "Magdalen of St. Teresa," all interred in the name of Mary of Magdalene, the wealthy patron of Jesus Christ. Branded as a whore by Pope Gregory *the Great* in AD 591. Magdalene the mystic, our Apostle 13, and the obvious chosen successor of Jesus—learned priestess the patriarchs of the church were compelled to demonize.

Sinéad's anger in song and her spoken words were not retributive; she did not advocate for payback to the criminal oppressors, but instead she was an illuminator, demanding that we look, we acknowledge, and in doing so, attempt to restore a sense of dignity to the oppressed. In an interview with *Time* magazine,[13] Martha Nussbaum talks about Martin Luther King Jr.'s philosophy of anger:

> "...what he thought is that you need to focus on the dignity of the people who suffered, and the dignity of their complaint and their outrage, but the retributive part

---

[12]Bernadette Devlin (McAliskey) is an Irish civil rights leader and former politician. Excerpt from an interview for *The Blindboy Podcast*, Season 1, Ep. 58, November 13, 2018.

[13]*Time Magazine*, July 19, 2018, Martha Nussbaum interviewed by Lily Rothman.

is not part of that. He said their anger must be "purified" and "channelized," he used those two words—meaning, we keep the outrage, and we keep the courage, but the retributive part about causing a lot of pain isn't very helpful. You have to turn to the future and think which emotions will actually help us solve the problem."

Warning: Don't drive west on Sunset Boulevard if you are susceptible to stimuli-induced seizures. The main drag of Sunset Boulevard in Los Angeles now resembles Las Vegas on crack. Lined with towering digital and electronic billboards, stroke-inducing flashes of images flip every few seconds at full-tilt visual scream. In September of 2023, I was accosted by a series of threatening billboards, some as large as 20 feet tall and 50 feet wide, featuring the lurid face of a monstrous, bloodless nun. Her Black Dahlia grin leering from behind a confession booth grid, she wears the white bandeau, guimpe, and coif beneath the black veil, the uniform of Catholic humility. Meet the ubiquitous cruel nun ad extremum, a hollow-eyed demon daring you to "confess your sins" as prelude to eating your soul. Another billboard on Hollywood Boulevard featured a three-dimensional church arch framing the demented sister from Hell. She commanded the LA streets for weeks. I couldn't escape her, reminding me of my darkest experiences with nuns, and that the best of charity in the Magdalene institutions was keeping girls alive with the least crumbs given after being discarded by their families. Of charity and refuge meant hardly that for girls and women. We were the disposables. No charity for refuse is more fitting—except in the cases where one good nun made all the difference. And there is always at least one good nun.

The billboards on Sunset were for *The Nun II* (sequel to *The Nun,* continuance of *The Conjuring* universe), which brought in $268 million worldwide. Spoiler alert: the inciting action is a repugnant nun's murder of a kindly priest. *The Nun II* eclipsed *The Equalizer 3* globally, released on the same date, starring Denzel Washington as an avenging angel. Does this point to an audience preference for evil women abusing good men? Or the preferences of Hollywood gatekeepers? Nasty Sisters of the Cloth far outweigh films with evil priests in theological horror movies. Our unholy sisters even have their own genre—Nunsploitation. Do an IMDb list search and you'll find "Nun Horror Films," but good luck on your nearly futile search for horror films about priests. I found no fewer than thirty nun horror flicks and suspect that's just the tip of the crucifix. Interesting fact—when I scanned YouTube for video news clips and docs about pedophile priests, I had to stop scrolling at 200+ entries, and on Google News, also stopped counting—tens of thousands of reports worldwide about sexual abuse in the Catholic Church, with male priests committing the horrors, compared to a handful of reports about nuns sexually abusing children in their care. Yet where are the movies about priestly pedophilia? Very few and far between. Even the high-profile cases are not considered worthy of feature films.

For instance, there's the case of George Pell, the Australian cardinal, archbishop of Melbourne, and senior Vatican figure. Australia's Royal Commission into Institutional Responses to Child Sexual Abuse in 2020 found that Pell knew of child sexual abuse by clergy in the 1970s but did not address it. The Commission stated that some 7 percent of priests (who worked in Australia between 1950 and 2009) were alleged perpetrators. (This finding did not represent allegations tested in a court of law.) The Vatican must have known. Pope John Paul II anointed Pell as cardinal in 2003. How long had Pell been covering up sexual abuse by pedophile priests in Australia? Committing these crimes against children himself? Pell was the most senior of all Vatican clerics to be convicted of child abuse and spent over a year imprisoned in solitary confinement in Australia. His convictions were overturned by Australia's High Court in 2020. It was Pope John Paul II's photo that Sinéad would tear apart on SNL.

The scary nun meme is chronic, and yes, there's some truth to the cliche, as the horrors of the Magdalen laundries have proven. Laundries aside, a hidden perversity lies within all this stereotyping. A fascination with the sadomasochistic aspects of Catholicism slithers throughout this campy abhorrence like a blooddrop of mercury let loose. Film critic on Roger Ebert's blog, Peyton Robinson, had this to say about *The Nun II*: "The paradoxical existence of a demonized sister of the cloth with horrifying sunken black eyes was an exciting promise."[14] Audiences thrill to stories of the sadistic nun and the lesbian nun, the latter never elevating beyond the gratuitous, far from authentic sex scenes. When I brought up the subject of nunsploitation movies versus the absence

---

[14]https://www.rogerebert.com/reviews/the-nun-ii-movie-review-2023.

of priestly horror films, a female friend exclaimed, "Well of course! Priests are *not hot!*"

Are all nuns wretched and cruel? This was neither Sinéad's nor my own experience, initially. Most of the time I spent with the Good Shepherds was one of discipline, yes, and of unexpected care and sweetness. As a child growing up in a schizophrenic home without any semblance of sanity or care, I felt safe inside the order and understand why Sinéad must have felt a sense of safe harbor. She'd been tortured by her abusive mother. An Grianán's Sister Margaret offered Sinéad a motherly tenderness. I imagine Sister Margaret's was a sober yet warm caring—the kind Sinéad had longed for but didn't deem possible. By discipline I do not mean punishment, but regulation and routine are necessary to a child's growth. Children without compassionate boundaries flounder; their edges evaporate in the salt water of tears.

Sister Margaret[15] purchased an acoustic guitar for Sinéad, an unlikely act in such an institution. The nun was obviously charmed by the quality of her singing voice, perhaps overheard as Sinéad caroled in a corner to a recording by Elkie Brooks of "Don't Cry Out Loud,"[16] made famous stateside by Melissa Manchester. Sister Margaret's nurturance mothered the birth of Sinéad's agency to make music. Sister Margaret also brought in a music teacher to show Sinéad how to place her fingers on the fretboard, matching the diagrams in the

---

[15]*Rememberings* by Sinéad O'Connor, p. 59.
[16]*Rememberings* by Sinéad O'Connor, p. 54.

Bob Dylan songbook gifted to her by the same nun. The first song she learned on guitar was Dylan's "To Ramona." The lyric counsels a girl to cease weeping over the dead and to stop trying to please a world that doesn't exist. It was the same Sister Margaret who sent Sinéad to an upstairs ward at An Grianán, to a secret world that should never have existed.

As punishment for some misdemeanor, the nun sent Sinéad to sleep upstairs with the ancient, sick women, Magdalens thrown away by their families with nowhere else to go. Some had lived in the laundry since they were wild girls. Others were quiet, unloved girls. Uncared for and too infirm to work, the older Magdalens were cloistered, their days and nights spent on dirty beds moaning for care, their bodies, hearts, and minds withering toward death. It scared the bee-Jaysus out of Sinéad and was meant to. I imagine Sister Margaret imagined this cruelty as a kindness, a warning to Sinéad that she must be good to ensure she'd not end up in the terrifying land of forgotten women. *Grow wings, girl, let the gift of your voice carry you away on the wind.* Soon after leaving An Grianán, Sinéad took flight with music as the sole wing strong enough to buoy her in the wind. But try as she might, she could not hide nor heal her broken wing.

Sister Margaret knew the forgotten women—no doubt knew about the trafficking of babies. The slogan of ACT UP/Aids activism rings true for so many social justice causes: silence = death. We know, too, what's truly happening. Feeling helpless, we grow numb, complicit in the terrible offenses of our time. This strange cruelty we're experiencing in our current body politic is deeply disturbing to the point of rearranging our neural pathways into dangerous territories via social media and the hypnotic scroll. In America as I write, a woman's autonomy over her own body has been taken away by misogynistic male and female politicians, and many poor women will literally die or suffer psychic death because of complicated and unwanted pregnancies. Is women's rage loud enough?

Ireland's ghost mothers and babies appear in the shimmering reverberations of Sinéad's miraculous voice. The shame of the imposter mother-nuns of Bon Secour snaking through the agonized cries of the elderly disposables of An Grianán, the 80,000-plus Magdalens, the Tuam babies, and the haunt of mother Marie O'Connor; I listen. I hear them. Sinéad's ever-present fantôme mother Marie shadows the entire LP, as she does many other Sinéad LPs. On *I Do Not Want What I Haven't Got*, Sinéad is stretched on her grave in a dirge-like mantra of a seventeenth-century Irish poem. She has stated many times how she's always singing about, and to, her mother, as she is doing on this LP.

Imagine an army of ghost mothers pushing you forward to sing for the unspoken. To liberate and release the buried pain, the loss, and the longing. To be a wing soaring in a soft blue sky of compassion. I imagine her there now. At peace.

I'M
NOT NO
ANIMAL IN THE ZOO
I AM WAITING FOR YOU AND THERE'S
ONLY ONE WAY TO BE FREE ALL IN ALL
IS ALL WE ALL ARE LIFE'S BACKWARDS
WE'VE MADE KILLERS OF OURSELVES
LET TEARS FALL LIKE EVERY LOVER
LA LA LA LA LA IRRELEVANT ANGELS
OR HAVE WE REALLY TRIED
WHEN YOU COULD HAVE DIED
WE MUST NOT, NOW OR
EVER IN THE FUTURE
MAKE POLITICS
MEMORY
MEMORY
MAKE POLITICS
EVER IN THE FUTURE
WE MUST NOT, NOW OR
WHEN YOU COULD HAVE DIED
OR HAVE WE REALLY TRIED
LA LA LA LA LA IRRELEVANT ANGELS
LET TEARS FALL LIKE EVERY LOVER
WE'VE MADE KILLERS OF OURSELVES
IS ALL WE ALL ARE LIFE'S BACKWARDS
ONLY ONE WAY TO BE FREE ALL IN ALL
I AM WAITING FOR YOU AND THERE'S
ANIMAL IN THE ZOO
NOT NO
I'M

5
Of Madness and Mother Courage

The monster I kill every day is the monster of realism.
The monster who attacks me every day is destruction.
Out of the duel comes the transformation.
I turn destruction into creation over and over again.[1]

—*Anaïs Nin*

You only have to look at the Medusa straight on to see her.
And she's not deadly. She's beautiful and she's laughing.

—*Hélène Cixous*
The Laugh of the Medusa

The hysteria of the madwoman's laugh rings throughout history. When we strip off the masks that confine our rage to expose the pain of our trauma, our inner Medusas tear the laces off the corseted. Mental illness is the most terrifying

---

[1]From "A Journal of Love": The Unexpurgated Diary of Anaïs Nin, 1931-1932, https://www.goodreads.com/book/show/11038.Henry_and_June.

inner scream released, the true cracking of the reality egg begging for recognition. Sinéad lived maskless. She spoke defiantly and exposed her vulnerable fragility just as often while calling out a corrupt world where women who protest are punished, cancelled, and labeled crazy. She knew what she was in for and did it anyway. She made us uncomfortable with the hypocrisy we feel we must abide and gave us a rare and authentic public view into what she freely called her mental illness, revealing a despair of a type that millions of people struggle with, yet dare not speak of for fear of being shamed as mentally ill. From the onset of rock stardom to her YouTube confessions and exploitation by Dr. Phil, Sinéad's trajectory toward mental illness was a slow build, the seeds having been sown in childhood as recounted on this LP. "Mental illness" sometimes proves physically spectacular and entertainment worthy for the exploiters, but the cost to those struggling is insurmountable. For Sinéad, public flogging took its toll.

I remember when she posted a video in 2017 on YouTube during what may have been her moment of darkest despair. This was twenty-four years after the release of *Universal Mother*, and I'll never forget the comments on that video—horrifying epithets and jokes expressing disgust, condemning and shaming her. In an extremely rare act of morality, YouTube removed most of the attacks, but the video is still up and is soul-crushing—Sinéad in a box on your computer, phone, and TV screen. Emotional wounds bleeding in living color with no tourniquet in sight. It was excruciating to witness a woman who refused to be boxed, labeled as Crazy Bald Head and stoned close to death on the public square in such agony. But she wanted us to see how it felt to be in excruciating mental anguish. She wanted to reach those who also suffer. To let them know they are not alone.

> One of millions, one of fucking millions . . . why are we alone? . . . the most vulnerable people on earth, we can't take care of our fucking selves. I gave so much love in my life and I just can't understand how a person can be left alone . . . mental illness, it's a bit like drugs. It doesn't give a shit about who you are . . . and equally you know what's worse is the stigma doesn't give a shit who you are. I'm fighting fighting fighting . . . I'm not staying alive for me. If it was me I'd be gone, straight away back to my mom.[2]

She makes a comment about all the "big hairy men" in her family who are "so scared of the little woman sending them angry emails." She admonished the fathers of her children, even railed about John Reynolds not responding to her (after she sent him a barrage of angry emails). She talked about a very valid truth concerning mental illness—that once you've been slapped with the label, everything you think, say, and feel is invalidated. "It's the stigma that's killing us, not the mental illness." She brought up her son Shane but not by name—how she was allowed to see her ten-year-old but not her thirteen-year-old (Shane) and how nuts that was in terms of the Irish custody laws. She kept saying she wanted to stay alive for her children. She was begging for someone to come and get her, to take her home. It was John Reynolds who came to her rescue.

---

[2] https://www.youtube.com/watch?v=yg5Z-8FWEYE&rco=1.

John told me when he arrived in the States, she met him at the airport laughing. Told him it was all an act, that she did it for show. She was not actually living in a Travel Lodge, but she rented the room to make the video. Yet it is obvious she was feeling what she expressed. Hers was not a performance. The two of them spent a few days in a New York hotel, ordered takeout, talked and laughed. And then John brought her home.

Sinéad has been very careful about covering her tracks when it comes to speaking about family members. When she's said things like what she expressed in this particular video, comments about family were usually followed by disclaimers. No matter how much distance her family kept from her and despite how abandoned she felt, she was protective of her family and never wanted to hurt anyone. She had no obligation to tell us details about her family members or what they may have gone through.

I'm sure she was thinking about herself and her mother when she wondered aloud if a person was born with mental illness or is made mentally ill. I'll go with the latter. Sinéad was cross-diagnosed and medicated for several psychological disorders—depression, bipolar disorder, borderline personality disorder, and complex PTSD. That she struggled with intimacy due to a childhood of abuse is not surprising. Her relationships were difficult. She alienated friends and family in a dramatic dance of extremes. She was incredibly loving, especially to her children, and often hilarious. But as it is with people who suffer from BPD, the wrong written word or a misconstrued expression on your face could flip her into fear, and sometimes with the result of that fear manifesting as rage. The fear of being unloved when you were unloved as a child can be extreme, can be a provocateur of anger.

There are hundreds of books, journals (both medical and scholarly), compilations, articles, essays, and theories on the concept of hysteria, and it is nearly impossible to read anything on the subject without the author pointing to the late-nineteenth-century French neurologist Jean-Martin Charcot and his photographs of patients at Salpêtrière hospital in Paris. Aside from his main subject, Louise Augustine Gleizes, most of Charcot's women patients are anonymous; Charcot supersedes his vassals.[3] He is both maestro and big daddy of hysteria as performance, maker of the photographic boxes that contained the "sick women" (as did another carnival barker 130 years later, Dr. Phil). It doesn't matter that Charcot was an esteemed neurologist; he presented his subject's curated contortions like freaks caught mid-act in a 5-penny circus. These images continue to enthrall the elite art world and academia today, who prefer Charcot's intellectual analysis of *Le grand asile de la misère humaine* to daytime television's capture of authentic women's suffering. With his cloying, faux empathy, and thirst for exposing the weak, Dr. Phil prodded, then showcased, a broken Sinéad to the ordinary world via electronic box, her pain pimped for ratings.

In an interview with Dr. Phil in 2017, O'Connor revealed that she'd attempted suicide no less than eight times in one year.

---

[3] Interview with Cindy Rehm, artist and educator.

"What kicked all of this off really was, I had a radical hysterectomy in Ireland two years ago and I lost my mind after that," she said, And that's what I think happened with my family, and we have to give my family credit. They're not here to speak for themselves so I don't want to disrespect them, but the fact is, they didn't know who the hell I was . . . I was told to leave the hospital two days after the surgery with Tylenol and no hormone replacement and no guidance as to what might happen to me. I was flung into surgical menopause. Hormones were everywhere. I became very suicidal. I was a basket case. After the hysterectomy, I was mental.

Hysteria was originally defined as a functional disruption of the nervous system due to a *disturbance of the uterine functions*. That is, hysteria was a state only biologically born women experience. Hysteria. Hysterical. Hysterectomy. The artist Cindy Rehm's work and study share a focus on hysteria that I found resonant with Sinéad's music and performance. Rehm states:

In hysteria and during séances, the female body becomes a conduit, a channel to release interior experiences to the external world. This also relates to ideas of the leaky body, that women are porous, that they expel blood, milk, and other bodily fluids. The porosity works the other way too[4]

Oh the horrors of the female body! The give and the take can break the brain.

---

[4] Cindy Rehm interview by Johanna Braun, from Hysterical Methodologies in the Arts, Stanford University, p. 174.

Sinéad's mental illness did not prevent her from caring deeply about the suffering of the world. In fact, her mental fragility seemed to enhance her compassion for others. She used the negativity around women and madness to her advantage. I believe she felt similarly to the way I felt about my own abusive mother, whose schizophrenia could be both phantasmagorical and exceedingly abusive. As much as I despised my mother's cruelty and abandonment, her illness taught me to see beyond the veil of this world and into the etheric. To embrace imagination. I have learned to wear her affliction as a badge of honor, a means of escape from the straitjackets that confine our imaginations. *Universal Mother* leaks the somatic fluids of Sinéad's womb-heart and maternal lineage. Equally, her porosity absorbed the pain inflicted on her as well as the suffering of others. Far beyond all man-made diagnoses, Sinéad was an empath, bringing us with her on an endless search for naming and healing.

There's a method to my own madness here. I'm bringing up the crazy because of the torment she endured at the hands of the press and public *after* the SNL incident and *before* she recorded *Universal Mother*. She was desperately in need of healing. These are the songs she wrote during the in-between. And it was John Reynolds who listened. It didn't take her long to give birth to these songs, considering the unwarranted punishment she had to endure for those two years after SNL. Her healing through songwriting commenced quickly. She did not lay around playing the victim. She got to work.

Being in a relationship with someone who suffers from mental illness is not for the cowardly. Reality is constantly warping, and you never know what is coming next; the instability wrecks the nerves if one isn't strong enough to maintain a core insight that the sufferer is not malicious and is merely frightened to death by perceptions of possible abuse and abandonment. During a conversation with John Reynolds, I learned why it was John who stood by Sinéad through the years, facilitated her making of music, rescued her when she was in need, and continued to be her rock, her most calming influence.

John Reynolds and Sinéad married in 1987 and had a child, Jake, that same year, and they've always shared the care of Jake. Jake, who sings "Am I Human?" on the LP, is her first—the only child of her four who was not taken away in a custody battle. During an interview for her last LP, she talked about how she and John "always loved each other since I was about 19. We always got on like brother and sister, which is why we didn't stay married."[5]

John Reynolds is an Irishman. His parents both worked in nursing and mental health care, and they decided to relocate the family to England near Oxford, for work. His parents found a huge house and converted it into a children's home, taking in up to thirty-six kids at a time—young kids lost in the system, abandoned, and troubled. Too young to be jailed for acting out, they were given safe harbor with the Reynolds. John grew up with these kids, shared a room with seven rescued boys inside this big, protective family. The kids all loved the Reynolds, and John says he stays in

[5] *Sunday World*, July 29, 2023, by Eddie Rowley.
https://www.sundayworld.com/showbiz/music/how-Sinéad-oconnors-love-for-first-husband-john-reynolds-lasted-a-lifetime/a722920883.html.

touch with many of his foster siblings. This upbringing of knowing and living intimately with troubled kids helped him tremendously in his relationship with Sinéad. To know the root of the erratic, sometimes destructive behavior is the lack of love and the fear of never having it opens the way for compassionate understanding.

> John: "It really helped. Most people would run away at one point. It didn't frighten me, I was used to crazy kids, had grown up with them from nine years old in our home. I had experienced similar emotional journeys with those siblings. Growing up that way also helped with the music . . . Sinéad and I had such determination that we were going to get the records right, we were going to stick at this. Even when we'd been married and then weren't married, the records somehow seemed more important. It's where we were happiest, I suppose, in the studio. Our relationship would never have lasted if I'd not grown up in that kid's home, had that experience."

What happens when a woman has a hysterectomy in the pre-menopausal years? Surgical menopause can be savage. Without a doctor's care administering the correct balance of bioidentical hormones and counseling before and after, body and soul are slammed into immediate menopause. Every woman who has experienced an organic menopause understands the gradual lead-up to the final termination and its aftermath as brutal and confusing enough. Sinéad had what she called a "radical hysterectomy" in 2015. Simon Napier-Bell, who managed Sinéad briefly, recalls her suffering from endometriosis as the reason for her hysterectomy. The definition of a radical hysterectomy is the surgical removal of the uterus, the cervix, the fallopian tubes, and the ovaries. Nearby lymph nodes and tissues are also excised. The ordinary hysterectomy (womb removal) causes changes in hormones and in the body, but the radical version causes rapid aging and can lead to coronary heart disease, stroke, and depression. Sinéad's physical and mental health took a turn for the worse after this surgery, also due to the hospital and the doctors refusing to administer hormone replacement therapy. If only she'd had a smart older woman looking after her. She needed a tender medical advocate.

Sinéad says 2015 was also the year her third child, Shane, began showing signs of emotional distress. Shane, whose father took custody away from Sinéad, committed suicide in 2022. He'd gone missing from Tallaght Hospital in Dublin where he was on suicide watch. She'd sent a number of tweets, begging Shane to turn himself into the Gardai. Several days after he was reported missing, Shane's body was recovered in Bray. Eighteen months later, his mother left this earth to join him.

Mother Courage is one of the many plays written by Bertolt Brecht in resistance to the rise of the Nazis in Germany.[6] Like Bertolt Brecht's character Mother Courage, Sinéad O'Connor lost her other three children, not to death by war, but by another kind of war. My own mother gave up

[6]It has recently come to light that the play was co-written by Margarete Steffin, who never received credit. https://en.wikipedia.org/wiki/Margarete _Steffin

her three children to the state due to her mental illness. And I can barely remember the ghost of her singing a lullaby.

On a search for the lyrics to the lullaby song in Bertolt Brecht's *Mother Courage*, I came across a Scottish translation from the German. Weans (wee-uns) is Scottish and Irish slang for children, pronounced "the wains" in Northern Ireland. It is the weans Mother Courage sings of as she holds her dead child in her arms:

> hushaby ma dearie
> nestlin' in the hay
> neighbours' weans are girnin
> oors jist run an play
> neighbours weans are clatty
> oors are clean an neat
> lookin like an angel sae sweet.[7]

LOVE
I LOVED HER
WHAT ELSE COULD I WRITE
LONELY HOUSE HAS BURNED
HER EYES LIKE A WILD IRISH SEA
GOD HE'S A DAYDREAMER LIKE ME
ONLY ALLOWED TO EAT STARS STARS
STARS THE STARS THE STARS THE STARS
FEELING THE EMPTINESS INSIDE WHILE
THE IRISH PEOPLE STARVED COULD HAVE
DIED. CHOKING ON ASHES THE DEATHS ON
SHIPS SAILING SAILING ON THIS TERRIBLE
OCEAN. WHERE DO THEY ALL COME FROM
BORN INTO GREAT PAIN SURROUNDED BY
DESPAIR THE PARENT FIGURES LIED TO US AND
MY BODY IS BREAKING MY HEART. WORSHIP GOD AS
A MOTHER OVER AND OVER FOR NO ONE REMEMBERS
GOD'S NAME. YOUR NAME'S A WHISPER. THAT ANY OF YOU
WILL FACE THE FUTURE THESE ARE THE WAYS OF LEAPING
UP AND GETTING YOU.
I'VE COME
FOR MYSELF
TO THE
SUN

6
Mother Ireland

I see the Irish as a race
like a child that got itself
bashed in the face.

—Sinéad O'Connor,
Famine

The spirit of Ireland fueled the bloodstream of Sinéad O'Connor, of her music, and certainly this LP. She once referred to *Universal Mother* as a "prayer from Ireland." Her music made me aware of an existential ache (hers, and my own) for historical roots, for an Irish language, culture, mythology, and history. I'm learning now and will preface my view of Sinéad as the metaphorical voice of Mother Ireland with a brief, and somewhat naïf, history lesson. I'll be avoiding "the Troubles."[1] Most of my Irish friends won't even attempt to explain its tangle-wreck of complications.

---

[1]The Troubles is a descriptor of the thirty-year period of conflict in Northern Ireland from the late 1960s to 1998's Good Friday Agreement. The origins of the Troubles go back hundreds of years.

A tricky epithet, Mother Ireland. Irish feminist filmmaker Pat Murphy spoke about this image of "woman as country" as won, colonized. Men being the pioneers, and:

> the weird psychological thing where the country is a woman, and you talk about the rape of a country and the rape of a woman. Again, women aren't seen for themselves, they're absolved into this overall mythology which is not a progressive one . . . For me, growing up it meant a very repressive image. It meant the weeping woman with the harp. It meant a particularly Irish version of the Virgin Mary. It always seemed to mean something that the church and other people were telling women what they should be.

Bernadette Devlin feels this image suits Ireland politically:

> If you look at aggressive countries and imperialist countries, they tend to be male countries . . . the German Fatherland, and America is a Fatherland. People that have a long history of oppression tend to think of their country in terms of Motherland. And in its own unconscious way, I think that is an acceptance of, the analogy of, oppression, and the oppression of women. So, I don't think it's a bad image.[2]

---

[2]Pat Murphy and Bernadette Devlin McAliskey are quoted from the documentary film *Mother Ireland*, directed by Anne Crilly, on the relationship between Irish women, nationalism, and republicanism. The film was originally deemed untransmittable under government restrictions imposed in October 1988. Devlin was shot nine times by the UDA (allegedly in collaboration with the British supposedly guarding Devlin) in front of

I've read several versions of England's rule over Ireland, one stating that it began in 1169 with the Anglo-Norman invasion. The 1800 Act of Union merged Ireland into a combined United Kingdom as it became one of Great Britain's extensive network of colonies. For most of the nineteenth century Great Britain was the largest, richest empire on earth, and once colonized, Ireland's farmers were forced to provide grains, livestock, dairy, vegetables, and other commodities to England, including wood (deforestation began in earnest in the sixteenth century under Elizabeth I) and the banning of Irish harp music. (Cruel Queen Lizzie again, who proclaimed in 1603 "to hang the harpers wherever found, and destroy their instruments." She wanted the harps burned—the harp had become a symbol of resistance to the Crown. A hair-raising story of its own.)[3] [4]

During An Gorta Mór (The Great Hunger), which lasted for more than seven years due to decades of food being exported to England, more than half the population of Ireland depended on potato crops. The killing blow came via a fungus that struck the potato crops in 1845. Over a million Irish people died during An Gorta Mór, aka the Famine.

her children. She survived. The Ulster Defence Association often attacked Catholics, partly in retaliation for Republican paramilitary actions.

[3]https://www.wirestrungharp.com/harps/harpers/dictates_against_harpers .html.

[4]https://www.irishcentral.com/roots/history/symbol-ireland-irish-harps -music-myth.

In 1847, thirty-six cargo ships not meant for human passengers made the journey across the Atlantic, down the Saint Lawrence seaway carrying 120,000 Irish immigrants in a massive emigration. The Irish "coffin ships" arrived at Grosse Ile, Quebec, waiting to unload not only healthy passengers but also the sick and the dead. At least a quarter of the Irish who died en route were thrown overboard on the journey. (That year is known as Black '47, mentioned in the song "Famine.") Among the healthy passengers were my mother's ancestors, who first settled in Halifax, Nova Scotia. Many Irish children lived in workhouses, orphaned by parents sacrificing their own sustenance to save their children's lives.

> And then, in the middle of all this
> They gave us money not to teach our children Irish
> And so we lost our history
> And this is what I think is still hurting me.

Irish children in the nineteenth century were forced to wear tally sticks (the *bata scór*) tied around their necks with string as punishment, and a notch was cut into the stick each time they were caught uttering an Irish word.[5] These are some of the wounds Sinéad speaks to when she asks for Irish remembering and grieving, as prerequisites to healing.

The reviews panning this LP expose the writers as feeling a need to engage in heartless perversions of Sinéad's intentions. So many of the reviews refer to "Famine" with a bit of a sneer as a rap or a hip-hop number. Although it does have a hip-to-

---

[5]https://www.askaboutireland.ie/learning-zone/primary-students/looking-at-places/meath/fr.-eugene-ogrowney/the-irish-language-in-the-1/.

trip-hoppy feel, it's too easy to bind songs up in specific genre boxes. The song itself cannot be diminished by muso-speak brackets. It created quite a bit of controversy in England for its scathing attack on the colonizer. And although Sinéad resonated deeply with various oppressions, she never tried to sound black, even when singing reggae. Her voice is never imitative; it is always hers alone.

Irish people have been doing spoken word/storytelling since AD 500, and "Famine" presents Sinéad as a *seanchaí*,[6] a traveling Irish storyteller carrying the history forward. "Famine" is spoken-word laid on top of a groove that could be considered trip-hoppy but the wolves howling, the classical violin and jazzy horn samples, and the sung "Eleanor Rigby" chorus and Sinéad's accent, create a weave that sounds unlike any rap song I've yet to hear. The influence of Tim Simenon's collage approach, which he employed to great effect with Bomb the Bass (Simenon is coproducer on the track), is evident here and works well with John Reynolds's sonic perspective to Sinéad's style. Simenon was partially responsible for Neneh Cherry's hit, "Buffalo Stance," Neneh's breakout single released in 1988 and a track on her debut LP *Raw Like Sushi*. You couldn't hit a dance floor in any major urban city without hearing multitudinous remixes of this track, also a reference to Malcolm McLaren's 1982 track "Buffalo Gals" from which it samples.

Fun anecdote; when Neneh performed the track on Top of the Pops, she was pregnant, and a reporter asked her if

---

[6]A *seanchaí* is a traditional Gaelic storyteller. Custodians of history, traveling with the news from place to place.

she would be "safe" performing pregnant. She replied, "Yes of course! It's not an illness!" (Sinéad performed pregnant many times over the course of her career and was initially counseled to abort by the suits at Chrysalis and Ensign during the making of her debut LP.)

As is the case with most of the songs on *Universal Mother*, "Famine" cycles back and forth between two chords. For a suite filled with *suantrai* (lullabies), rage, and grief, I imagine Sinéad wanting at least one track that swung; Simenon's style was the perfect fit, bringing a bedrock rhythm to anchor her agit-prop poetics. Throw down some truths, she does just that in the name of all the lonely people. Sinéad might veil her beliefs in the simplest of prayers, but deep down she feels the subjugation of women to be at the root of all the troubles, and not just those of Northern Ireland: "We used to worship God as a Mother; now look at what we're doing to each other."[7]

The fiddle sample in the song's intro is from the film *Fiddler on the Roof*, as is the sample speaking of tradition from the film's main character, Tevye, that closes the song. The other male voice that comes in about three minutes forty seconds is Irish prime minister Jack Lynch, pulled from a speech on the Troubles from 1970.[8]

"We stand on the brink of a great achievement. In this Island, there is no solution to be found, to our disagreements, by shooting each other. There is no real invader here. We are

---

[7]From the song Sinéad O'Connor, "Famine," *Universal Mother*.
[8]https://www.songfacts.com/facts/Sinéad-oconnor/famine.

all Irish, all our different kinds of ways. We must not now, and ever in the future, show anything to each other except tolerance, forbearance, and neighbourly love."

The record's songs and her choices of text on the CD booklet place Sinéad as feeling that a return to the pagan, mother-centered religion of Irish history could be its saving grace. If the children were taught true Irish history, language, and culture, combined with a reverence for the Mother, this could heal the rift between Protestant and Catholic, English and Irish, women and men, in the spirit of fraternity that opens the album.

How can anyone listen to the song "In This Heart" and not hear the voice of Mother Ireland in all her vulnerability and noble strength? The longing and love, the desire for connection is palpable, as is the Irishness of the melody and the harmonies. Hearing the song for the first time stopped my heart. John Reynolds and Sinéad had recorded a lot together before this LP. He felt she'd been carrying the songs on *Universal Mother* for years, saw them as pieces of literature, complex stories. All the top lines (the melodies) were there, and she just circled them around in her head, with no references, demos, or tapes. Her memorizing head and heart were the dual tape decks.

John told me a story about the making of "In This Heart," which Sinéad composed on her own and initially sang to him a cappella, in the tradition of deep ancient Irish music. They knew the song should begin solo, but they felt an Irish choir with its distinctive harmonies would bring it a more magical resonance. Initially, they brought gear to a church to record with the Irish choir Anúna, but the result was overarched. Too big and grand. The song needed a more intimate approach. Enter the Voice Squad, a traditional Irish singing group of three older gentlemen: Gerry Cullen, Phil Callery, and Fran McPhail. They join the song one at a time, each bringing his own harmony to Sinéad's lead. The result lives on as musical ecstasy. Phil Callery died in 2022. His performance with Sinéad and his singing friends will echo immortal love through the ethers.

In "A Perfect Indian," Sinéad sings, "Too long have I been feeling like Lir's children," a fifteenth-century Irish fable (the Children of Lir). The story goes that the stepmother of Lir's four children blamed them for her losing the affection of Lir and cursed them by turning them into swans exiled for 900 years, never to know their true home, yet still able to sing in their human voices. Sinéad's lyrics speak of the innocence of a baby boy, and one imagines, herself, as a baby girl. The song follows "All Apologies," an addendum to her feelings about Kurt Cobain.

An online search for photos of Cobain as a child yielded a shot of him at about eight years old dressed as a "perfect young Indian," with a single feather for a headdress. Blonde. Teeth aching. In America, Cobain grew up, as I did, playing cowboys and Indians, and the cowboys didn't always win. This was decades before talk of appropriation. Sinéad could also be referring to Daniel Day-Lewis who plays the white adopted son of Mohicans in the 1992 film *The Last of the Mohicans*, released two years before *Universal Mother*. Sinéad says the song was inspired by his performance. On Day-Lewis, Sinéad told the Irish Sun, "It's not that I was in love with him (I wasn't), but I was very fond of him as a friend. The song is as much about my upbringing as it is about Daniel." She admitted to ruining their friendship by losing her temper with him.

In the song, Sinéad compares the boy's face to the elf arrow of Irish and Scottish lore, a flint that can inflict mortal wounds without breaking the skin, created by elves and shot by witches. Maybe the boy and girl were the receivers of elf arrows, cursed as were the Children of Lir by the evil stepmother Aoife. Day-Lewis is Anglo-Irish and Kurt Cobain was of Irish origin. Cobain's ancestors were from County Tyrone, and his mother eventually married an O'Connor. Sinéad was writing and recording the songs for *Universal Mother* the year Cobain committed suicide. "There's only one way to be free," she sings.

Sinéad released "All Apologies" and *Universal Mother* on September 13, 1994, six months after Kurt Cobain's death. She was no stranger to the desire to leave this earth, having attempted suicide in 1993, a year after the SNL moment, and she clearly felt a kinship with Cobain. Like him, she didn't want the media attention, the fame (well, maybe the infamy), or she'd never have ripped up that photo of il Papo. Both were unlikely pop stars who struggled with mental health issues. When I was thinking about her reverent, shimmering cover of "All Apologies," I could only find one instance of Sinéad having met Kurt Cobain. Photos were taken of her in Los Angeles at Universal Amphitheater in September 1993 by Lisa Rose. Sinéad is with Kurt, Courtney Love, and their baby daughter Frances Bean. Another member of this small backstage gathering, keeping what appears to be a safe distance from Sinéad, is Peter Gabriel, who'd soon break her heart. Sinéad spoke of this meeting with Cobain: "I was feeling very sorry for him, and I couldn't tell you why, but I thought, 'oh my God. That's a man that's suffering.'"[9]

"All Apologies" speaks to her sense of resignation being in line with Cobain's; rock stardom makes a person the object of mass projection, and expectations you could never imagine to fill, no matter what. There's a subtle hint of sarcasm in keeping with the original, yet Sinéad brings something totally new to the haunting melody—a hushed, confessional submission, devastating in its fragility. In the September 1994 issue of Britain's *Q* magazine, the month of *Universal Mother*'s release, she told Phil Sutcliff: "I never want to go through what I have gone through in the last four years ever again." She wrote, "And I accept my own responsibility in all of it. I am very sorry for all the hurt that I have ever caused to anyone while on this journey. Of growing up." She wanted, needed, to atone and heal with this LP.

I hear her singing for Cobain and for herself, and I'm transfixed by their kindred feelings of not being able to live up to people's / and to fame's expectations / in the personal and public realms. Hers is the kemal voice of wisdom, with the etheric quality of the otherworldly. The only accompaniment is her subtle strumming of an acoustic guitar. Of all Sinéad's streaming songs, the only recording that beats "All Apologies" 34 million streams (as of this writing) is "Nothing Compares to You."

[9]https://www.metro.us/Sinéad-oconnor-talks-bossy-beyonce-sex-appeal-and-kurt-cobain/.

Sinéad's autobiography of songs on *Universal Mother* is a gift of intimacy—a kind of intimacy (into-me-see) that makes the critics, usually fellahs, squirm. But not the men who've been broken by these systems.

While working with Wayne Kramer's "Jail Guitar Doors," we brought songwriting workshops to male inmates at Twin Towers in downtown L.A. and to women at L.A. County's Lynwood Jail. The men freely expressed their stories through song, and were vulnerable and open. I'd walk out of some of those sessions in tears, moved by intimate song confessionals exposing how society's systemic oppressions can shift a man to dark turnings. The difference between the men and the women was heartbreaking—the young women were a much harder ticket. Most were extremely shut down, reluctant to express any feelings at all. Many were mothers. They had been abused in one way or another, their minds colonized into silence, their crimes often committed as vengeance against their abusers, who more often went scot-free. One young woman had the word "HATED" tattooed in huge letters on her neck. We could not coax a word from her.

Sinéad speaks for these women, for their unexpressed hurts and longings. One could say the colonization of Ireland and the attempted erasure of Irish culture can be read in the story of the Children of Lir, exiled from their own land. But the song of the swans never died. It lives on in the blessed words and notes of Sinéad. She sings to us with rage against the colonizers of land and mind, body and soul. She sings to us as broken, loving mother and abandoned child filled with longing. She sings as an activist for God—God as One Love, as Music, as the Holy Ghost in us all. As an activist she takes her place among the canon of Irish women rebels; St. Brigid of Kildare, Grace O'Malley the Pirate Queen, Constance Markievicz, Annie Besant, Lady Jane Wilde, Bernadette Devlin, Ann Devlin, Mary Doyle, and the list goes on and on to include many valiant women whose lives and brave acts have been obscured and overshadowed by hagiographers. With *Universal Mother*, Sinéad's anxiety of living in a lawless world is a woven braid of her personal pain, the sorrows of her country, and of women and mothers. It's a song-cycle embrace of Mother Ireland, vibrating merciful waves of sound in the waters surrounding her island womb.

SMILE

AT ME. LIKE
TOTAL ANARCHY
LIKE LIR'S CHILDREN
MY LOVE
TOO LONG HAVE I BEEN FEELING THERE'S
LOVE THERE'S ONLY LOVE IN THIS WORLD
BUT WE'VE LOST CONTACT WITH OUR HISTORY
AND IF THERE IS EVER GONNA BE HEALING
OF A MOTHER WHO CAN'T UNDERSTAND
THERE HAS TO BE REMEMBERING
FLOWN FROM THE UNIVERSE
ALL THE LONELY PEOPLE
WITH THE GOLDEN HAIR
RED CHEEKS AND ON DRUGS
WHO LIVED IN A CAGE FRIGHTENED
BY A TERRIBLE BROKEN HEART
FIND MY NEST OF SALT
THE FIRE IS STILL HURTING ME
LIFTED BY THE HANDS OF
ME LITTLE STREET FIGHTER
I WILL HAVE YOU WITH ME
LITTLE DANCER
ALL APOLOGIES
SO LET'S TAKE A LOOK SHALL WE?
ON THE DAY
MY MOTHER WAS BURIED
MY GRIEF, MY GRIEF, MY GRIEF
THIS IS WHAT YOU FIND
DONT BE AFRAID

TO CRY

Epilogue
Thank You for Hearing Me

The closing track of *Universal Mother* is a mantra of gratitude, a hymn set to a pulsing, hypnotic bass line and groove. It's Sinéad at her most humble and passionate, the perfect denouement to her opera of healing, tenderness, and hard-earned wisdom. Many critics thought it was a break-up song about Peter Gabriel, but that gives the man too much credit. She is thanking all of us that stuck by her through the storms, who have listened to this LP and her music and her song-prayers all along. She's thanking John Reynolds for being her rock, thanking her lovers and her heartbreakers (Gabriel among them) for making her stronger. Thanking all who've shown her compassion and tenderness during a fury of a time in her life. The song builds into a more powerful vocal expression to the finale of thanking the one (or ones) for breaking her heart. She cowrote the song with John and coproduced with Tim Simenon, hence the track's touch of hip-hop. But again, her crystalline vocal expression is distinctly Irish. Interestingly, the song was released as a single and performed best in Iceland, where it hit #5 on the chart. It did fairly well in the United Kingdom, top 20, but the single completely eluded the US pop charts, much to the chagrin of the suits at Chrysalis USA who raked in a fortune from her previous LP's and singles.

The music video for "Thank You . . ." is a re-birthing metaphor. It begins with Sinéad's startling eyes in extreme close-up, the camera pulling out to reveal she is naked but not suggestively so, her body curled into a near-fetal position. An egg appears, half of it in light, the other half shrouded in darkness. On returning to her revolving image, her mid-torso seems bound and bandaged but not in a restrictive way as she appears inside the egg, holding herself protectively while thanking us for staying with her. In the last verse, as she wails a thanks for breaking her heart, she is released from the egg and floats away, caressed by clouds. Her voice dips back into a soft whisper, and she dissolves, becoming one with the empyrean.

Sinéad dedicated *Universal Mother* as "a prayer from Ireland . . . and with love and gratitude to my sister Eimear and my son Jake." Inside the CD booklet of *Universal Mother*, Sinéad the witch quotes from a Wiccan prayer, The Charge of the Goddess:

She says,

Whenever ye have need of anything, once in the month, and better to be when the moon is full, then shall ye assemble in some secret place: to thee I shall teach things that are yet unknown, and ye shall be free from all slavery. Keep your honest ideal. Strive ever toward it, let nothing stop you nor turn you aside. Mine is the cup of the wine of life, and the cauldron of Cerridwen. I am the Mother of all living and my love is poured out on the earth, the white moon among the stars, and the mystery of the waters, and the desire in the heart of Woman. Before my face let thine innermost divine self be enfolded in the raptures of the infinite. Know the mystery, that if that which thou seekest thou findest not within thee, thou wilt never find it without thee. For behold, I have been with thee from the beginning, and I await thee now. Blessed be.[1]

Ideals like harmony between the sexes, respect for nature, and coexistence without warfare are not just theoretical possibilities. They are realities of past societies. If only the men we need in the struggle could say the word "patriarchy" without fear and realize the true enemy. To understand the difference between patriarchy and masculinity is crucial: the evil of the former, the beauty and strength of the latter. And to bring back reverence for the Mother.

Sinéad was a mother martyr, publicly enduring the constant negative messaging that women are less-than and should never speak too loudly about their own, or the world's pain. We shouldn't use our public platforms to call out injustice, and if we do, we're labeled as crazies and ingrates (just look around at how few female celebrities dare speak truths about a myriad of oppressions). We should just "shut up and sing." We exist to be controlled and diminished blatantly and insidiously. In June 2022, America's Supreme Court overruled *Roe versus Wade*, making it extremely difficult for women to have abortions.

---

[1]https://www.learnreligions.com/charge-of-the-goddess-history-and-variations-4151704.

The overturn granted power to individual states to decide to criminalize women for aborting children under any circumstances, including pregnancies due to rape or when a pregnancy can prove fatal to the fetus or the mother. Currently, several states can legally demand, *Woman, do what you're told with your body. Face death by complicated pregnancies, still-born children, and other complications, or you're looking at incarceration.*

The ongoing war on women's bodies and psyches includes cultural messages that a woman's vagina is her most important asset, the female brain be damned. One of, if not the highest-grossing film of 2023, *Barbie*—cultural icon of plastic white American womanhood with feet anatomically disfigured in service to high heels—is a miasma of contradictory messages about feminism and gender roles. What may have initially been an exciting, provocative script was turned into Silly Putty by a cabal made up of suits at Mattel and the film's various producers. There's a lot of "poor Ken"-ing, and the one decent feminist speech delivered by a Latina firebrand is completely undone by her rebellious punk daughter transforming herself into an ultra-femme Barbie doll by the story's end. The second to last scene in *Barbie* features a soliloquy delivered to the doll from the God-like woman who created her at Mattel, about the importance of motherhood trumping all other female functions and desires. I'm all for motherhood. But—spoiler alert—the film concludes with the suddenly human Barbie marching into a business tower. We assume she's there to take her seat as CEO. Instead, she gleefully announces, "I'm here to see a gynecologist!" (i.e., *I have a pussy!*) If Sinéad the feminist was upset about Miley

Cyrus grinding away nearly naked on a wrecking ball, she'd have been apoplectic over *Barbie*. Cruel mothers often conspire with dominating fathers to diminish and oppress their own sex. And sometimes, their own daughters.

Social media is complicit in wrecking teenage girl's lives, with its white male tech masters refusing any culpability in the algorithmic wormholes that block contrary images and views. Once you travel down a path a few times, the exit proves elusive. Social media was also complicit in ruining Sinéad O'Connor's mental health via its highly addictive slot-machine scrolling. The dopamine must be potent for celebrities, since so many seem to post incessantly throughout the days and nights. It doesn't matter if it's assistants or AI doing the dirty work. The postings obsessively feed the female insecurity machine. The silent complicity of tech bros overseeing the messaging proves they want their women to be pretty and competitive with each other—desirable to men, envious of the next scrolled femme "influencer."

You'll never see Mark Zuckerberg or Elon Musk speaking up for women's rights. Girls already socially wired to compete cannot contend with filtered images pushing manufactured beauty and thrilling, fun-filled lives. Lives doing what, exactly? Looking flawlessly hipster beautiful with fab friends in wildly fun locations? Every teen girl's competitive nightmare—that she will never be cool enough—is now on speed-dial via a scrolling personal slot machine where impossible masks taunt, *this is what you should aspire to in life!* It isn't a stretch to grasp how a child's perception of reality can become degradingly distorted by social media or by films that portray women and girls as less than, as objects of violence and murder. America's Centers for Disease Control (CDC) has been collecting data for thirty years on teen mental health and suicides, and the research shows that "Suicide has been the second-or third-leading cause of death for young people between 10 and 24 years for decades now," girls doubling the rate of teen boys by up to 60 percent from a decade ago.[2] And as of December 2023, Ireland has the highest rate in Europe for young girls taking their own lives.[3]

Days before Sinéad passed, she broke her sabbatical of posting videos of herself with a personal video on YouTube about her new flat in London and what she was up to. She was self-conscious about her looks, touching her face questioning / doubting / joking if she was still a sexual being. She called her flat a shithole through a dimpled smile, mentioned her son's suicide, and that she was planning to write new songs on her new guitar. Overall, she was a bit speedy bordering on manic, yet her sweetness and mischievous side shone. She hadn't posted any selfie videos in ages and was probably counseled to stay away from social media. Maybe she received nasty feedback in the comments of that last video. YouTube took down her original video post after she passed.

I've recently been granted the gift and the great responsibility of co-parenting a young girl, a toddler. I cringe at the thought of her innocence being damaged by absorbing

[2]https://www.pbs.org/newshour/health/cdc-data-shows-u-s-teen-girls-in
-crisis-with-unprecedented-rise-in-suicidal-behavior.

[3]https://www.independent.ie/life/health-wellbeing/mental-health/ireland
-has-the-highest-rate-in-europe-for-young-girls-taking-their-own-lives
/35527041.html.

negative messaging, both insidious and overt, about girls and women. I do not want her to ever feel less than, to silently agree to be subjugated in service to a system of harm, her mind and body legislated by politics and cultural ideologies. Imagine the cumulative effect of all this messaging on women and girls when combined with anthropological studies about woman's hostility toward other women; one such study states that 91 percent of the 137 international societies surveyed show women mainly targeting other women with their aggression.[4]

Despite decades of condemnation, bullying, and degradation by the press, Sinéad O'Connor kept returning to make work and to give us her otherworldly voice in words and music. Listen to her version of the gospel song "Trouble of the World" from 2020. Marie O'Connor rises again as Sinéad sings, "I want to see my mother." She is with her now. Blessed be.

Sinéad concludes the CD booklet for *Universal Mother* with an excerpt from a poem by W. B. Yeats. Fittingly prescient words from one Irish poet to another, to our pop star woman prophet:

Half close your eyelids, loosen your hair,
and dream about the great and their pride;
they have spoken against you everywhere,
but weigh this song with the great and their pride;
I made it out of a mouthful of air,
their children's children shall say they have lied.

[4]*Woman's Inhumanity to Woman* by Phyllis Chesler, p. 127.

Sinéad left us in a funeral procession along the seaside promenade in Bray, passing the house where she lived for many years—the house where she loved and lost her son Shane. Crowds gathered to pay tribute, some holding signs; one read "suffer little children" and suffer did many in Irish "care" homes and orphanages. Leading the procession was a vintage VW bus draped in the LGBTQ Rainbow Pride Flag, the Progress Pride Flag, and the Rasta flag—the green, yellow, and red colors Sinéad had painted on the cornerstones of her house in Bray. Inside the hearse, her coffin was covered in blue hydrangeas and pale pink roses, and as the procession made its way along the seafront, mourners tossed flowers onto the hearse. Mounted on top of the VW bus were loudspeakers playing a track from Bob Marley's LP *Exodus*, "Natural Mystic." *If you listen carefully now you will hear* the doors that death opens.

Sinéad lived our collective suffering in song. Exposing wounds too many of us have had to bear under the weight of Judeo-Christian patriarchy and its fear and oppression of women, she sings to us here, in the name of the *Universal Mother*. She did not give her life for us in vain.

OM SHANTI
AN DEIREADH

Acknowledgments

I'd like to thank Mary Gormley for her kindness in introducing me to John Reynolds. And to John, Sinéad's hero and rock, my deepest gratitude to you for your time and stories, and your ongoing care for Sinéad, Jake, and Yeshua. Your input to this book has been its greatest treasure. Vivienne Griffin, thanks for your stories, your signposts, and especially the history of the burning of the harps. Thank you, Pat Murphy, for inspiring me as a spiritual presence and as a filmmaker. Vivienne Dick, also for your films, the trip down to Bray, and our walk along the promenade. And thanks to my mother Kitty and our maternal Irish ancestors. You were with me through every moment and word. This book is also for you.

I wouldn't have made it through the process of making this book without the support of my partner dama and her daughter Maya, who fill my life with joy and deep gratitude. Obrigada to the artist dama for collaborating with me on the poem shapes. To my sister Natalie Hill and my inner circle— Liz Graves, Lizzie Borden, Nona Hendryx, Jack Ryan, Jeffrey Hill, and my Promises and Home Free families—thank you all for "seeing me and not leaving me." And thanks to the good men now gone who've inspired me on their earthly journeys: Hugh W. Harris, Peter Laughner, and Wayne Kramer.

Thank you, Leah-Babb Rosenfeld, 33 1/3rd, and Bloomsbury for the opportunity to make this book. To Evelyn McDonnell for mentorship and pointing me in Leah's direction. And the deepest gratitude to my brilliant editor, author and professor Samantha Bennett. Sam, you rock.

Most of all, thank you, Sinéad, for the music, the immensity of love you've given, and the constant magical reminders to stay on track—the hummingbirds, the nighttime knocks, and the broken bowl, which remains in two perfect pieces in my cupboard. I pray I've done right by you. And if not, I'm sure I'll be hearing about it.